Meet
PADRE PIO

Meet
PADRE PIO

Beloved Mystic, Miracle Worker, and Spiritual Guide

PATRICIA TREECE

CHARIS

SERVANT PUBLICATIONS
ANN ARBOR, MICHIGAN

Charis Books is an imprint of Servant Publications especially designed to serve Roman Catholics.

Published by Servant Publications
P.O. Box 8617
Ann Arbor, Michigan 48107

Cover design by Brian Fowler, DesignTeam-Grand Rapids, Michigan
Cover photograph of Padre Pio courtesy of The National Centre for Padre Pio, Barto, PA

02 03 04 10 9 8 7 6 5 4 3 2

Printed in the United States of America
ISBN 0-56955-249-5

Library of Congress Cataloging-in-Publication Data

Treece, Patricia.
    Meet Padre Pio : beloved mystic, miracle worker, and spiritual guide / Patricia Treece.
        p. cm.
    Includes bibliographical references.
    ISBN 1-56955-249-5 (alk. paper)
    1. Pio, padre, 1887-1968. 2 Capuchins—Italy—Biography. 3. Stigmatics—Italy—
Biography. 4. Catholic Church—Italy—Clergy—Biography. 5. Christian saints—
Italy—Biography.   I. Title.
    BX4700.P7755 T74 2001
    271' .3602—dc21

                                                                    2001032456

DEDICATION

*To all priests, brothers, deacons, and pastors everywhere
who are giving their lives to shepherd their flocks.*

And especially to my friends

*Fr. Joseph Elworthy, C.S.S.R.
and
Monsignor John V. Sheridan*

*Multitalented men whose lives,
rich in wisdom and understanding,
God's mercy and compassion,
have blessed our human family.*

He Was Like Every Boy

Teasing his sisters was always fun. Many times he snuck up behind two-years-younger Felicita as the little girl washed herself in the portable bathtub on the kitchen floor. With glee the future saint would dunk his little sister's head under the soapy water.

And like boys everywhere, at least once he took food meant for someone else—that time, when he was quite ill, he crept out of bed and devoured the entire platter of peppers his mother had cooked for the harvest hands. Only when she accused his older brother of letting the dog eat them did Franci* (as Padre Pio was then called) confess.

Every boy tries to smoke. Given money by a neighbor to go buy the man a cigar, on the way home, Franci lit up. One puff and he was sick to his stomach. That ended his smoking career.

*short for his baptismal name Francesco

He could plot revenge, too. On a hot summer afternoon a playmate, Mercurio Scocca, buried him under corn shocks as Franci lay sleeping beneath a tree during southern Italy's siesta time. Waking in darkness, Franci, scared, screamed for his mother, to the other boy's roars of laughter. The next day, Franci discovered Mercurio taking *his* siesta atop a small farm wagon. He pulled the wagon, with the sleeping Mercurio, up a nearby hill and shoved it over the crest. Mercurio suddenly wakened to the ride of his life. Fortunately for both boys, the hurtling wagon ran into a tree, which stopped it before the rider could be hurled off and injured.

Yet There Were Signs

Luigi Orlando, a contemporary who used to play with Franci and agrees "he was like any other boy," also recalls a day when they were wrestling. Franci pinned Luigi, who swore in exasperation. Immediately Franci released him and fled. He had been taught by his mother—and strictly followed her injunction—to leave immediately any place where bad language was used.

The child also loved to pray, which was not unusual in a family known as "the family for whom God is everything." Yet he went at it with an intensity that stood out even in the Forgione family: Local priest Father Giuseppe Orlando later remembered reprimanding the boy because he disobeyed his mother, who wanted him to sleep in his bed, while he preferred, penitentially, to sleep on the floor, using a stone for a pillow.

Franci, who had already told his parents he wanted to be a priest, also practiced self-flagellation. When his mother reproached him for beating himself, he replied, "I must beat myself the same way Jesus was beaten." Extremely devout, Giuseppa Forgione felt tears come to her eyes, she later said. From then on she did not interfere with this practice.

From the Beginning, So to Speak

Years later, in 1915, his spiritual director learned that from the age of five—when Francesco first had had the idea of consecrating himself forever to the Lord—the boy had had apparitions, seeing Jesus and the Virgin Mary primarily but also terrible, diabolical figures. Francesco never spoke of any of it, assuming everyone else also saw the things he did. Only after he had been some years in the Capuchins did he one day offhandedly query his spiritual director, "Don't you see the Madonna?" When the man said that he didn't, Pio immediately responded, "You're only saying this out of holy humility."

And then it all came out. Not only had Padre Pio had visions of Jesus, Mary, and devils, but as a child he saw his guardian angel so frequently that he referred to the angel fondly as "the playmate of my childhood." The guardian angel would play such a prominent role in Padre Pio's adult life that one of his Capuchin confreres would fill an entire book[1] with incidents where Padre Pio interacted with his own angel and the guardian angels of others.

He Suffered in Giving up the World

When he moved into adolescence, Francesco Forgione did not long for power, riches, sexual conquests, or wild living. Instead, it was the true riches the world offers that drew Franci: to remain with his family, so strong in their love for one another, and to seize the joys he had learned among them. Chief among these was family life itself, with its innocent pleasures of laughter, food, a glass of wine, sharing a good story, praying together, and, above all, knowing they were there for each other in good times and bad. To give up all this and leave the ones he so deeply loved to enter the Franciscans and study for the priesthood seemed beyond the fifteen-year-old's strength.

Christ came to comfort him during his last night at home. He later wrote under obedience to his spiritual director, speaking of his soul in the third person:

It saw Jesus and His Mother who, in all their majesty, began to encourage it and assure it of their predilection. Finally Jesus placed a hand on his head and that was enough to strengthen the upper part of the soul so as to avoid his shedding even one tear during the painful separation, despite the painful martyrdom which tore the body and soul.

The Whole of His Life

The whole of his life can be summed up in another vision from these final days before his entry into the Capuchin Franciscan[2] seminary. Meditating on his calling by God to become a priest, he suddenly had an unforgettable experience. From the account he wrote under obedience to his spiritual directors, speaking of himself, as always, in the third person:

He saw by his side a majestic man of rare beauty, splendid as the sun. This man took him by the hand and he heard him say: "Come with me, because you will have to fight as a valiant warrior."

Then he was led to an area of very spacious countryside. Here there was a great multitude of men divided into two groups. On one side he saw men of most beautiful countenance ... in snow-white garments. On the other ... men of hideous aspect, dressed in black like so many dark shadows.

As he stood between the two groups, a giant man appeared with his forehead seeming to touch the heavens and a face that was horrible.

This strange personage approached nearer and nearer and the guide who was beside the soul informed him that he would have to fight with that creature. At these words the poor little soul turned pale, trembled all over and was about to fall to the ground in a faint, so great was his terror.

The guide supported him with one arm until he recovered somewhat from his fright. The soul then turned to his guide and begged him to spare him from the fury of that eerie personage, because he said the man was so strong that the strength of all men combined would not be sufficient to fell him.

[The guide answered:] *"Your every resistance is vain. You must fight with this man. Take heart. Enter the combat with confidence. Go forth courageously. I shall be with you. In reward for your victory over him I will give you a shining crown..."*

The poor little soul took heart. He entered into combat with the formidable and mysterious being. The attack [of the giant being] *was ferocious but with the help of his guide, who never left his side,* [the soul] *overcame his adversary, threw him to the ground, and forced him to flee.*

As promised, a crown was placed on the soul for a moment but almost immediately it was removed and the guide said:

"I will reserve for you a crown even more beautiful if you fight the good fight with the being whom you have just fought. He will continually renew the assault to regain his lost honor. Fight valiantly and do not doubt my aid. Keep your eyes wide open, for that mysterious personage will try to take you by surprise. Do not fear his ... formidable might, but remember what I have promised you: that I will always be close at hand and I will always help you, so that you will always succeed in conquering him."

Now all the multitude who were in darkness and whose faces were also horrible after the defeat of the giant fled with shrieks, curses, and horrible cries while the other multitude praised and applauded *the splendid man more radiant than the sun who had assisted the poor soul so splendidly in the fierce battle. And so the vision ended.*

A day or so later a second spiritual experience confirmed that Francesco's whole life as a priest would require combat with his mysterious adversary from hell. Demons would be present at his battles to jeer, but he must never fear, for the angels would also be there to applaud his victories over the evil one. He understood furthermore that the heavenly guide was Jesus Christ himself, who would sustain him in the battle so long as he trusted in the Savior and fought valiantly.

A New Life Given Utterly to God

On January 6, 1903, fifteen-year-old Francesco Forgione left Pietrelcina with two other boys from his area. His mother, blessing him through her tears, said he belonged now no longer to her but to St. Francis. An hour's train ride brought him to the town of Morcone, where the boys found their way to the friary of Saints Philip and James. The door was opened by Franci's hero, Fra Camillo of S. Elia a Pianisi, who welcomed them warmly. This young friar had usually been the Capuchin sent out to beg in places like Pietrelcina, picking up not only eggs, grain, wine, and other foodstuffs, but the admiration of little boys as well. Francesco, for instance, spurned the other religious orders he might have entered because he insisted he wanted to have a beard, like Fra Camillo did.

Recovering from more than two decades of suppression by the Italian government, the Capuchins were mostly young and very fervent. Franci was shown to room 18, then after a short time moved to another tiny room (Capuchins call them cells), number 28, in the seminarians' corridor. Each cell had a straw mattress that rested on four planks and trestles, a very small table to hold the Bible and a few other books such as the *Imitation of Christ*, and a chair. On the wall was always a crucifix and Scriptures from both the Old and New Testaments.

One of the Scriptures in Pio's cell 28 was "You are dead and your lives are hidden with Christ in God." Given a new name symbolizing his new "birth" as one given utterly to God, Francesco Forgione would be known for the rest of his life as Pio. After an introductory period of just over two weeks, he began a year of novitiate under a novice master who was severe but also a man "with a heart of gold," full of charity and understanding for the young men he guided.

From the beginning, even the strictest Capuchin called Frater Pio[3] "an exemplary novice [who was] an example to all." While gluttony is a common problem to young men, Pio preferred prayer even to eating. Yet he was cheerful and down to earth, retaining his love of pranks and telling jokes when talking was allowed.

One of his pranks took place on a midnight when, as was their habit, the community arose from their beds to pray at a time when many sins take place. Returning from the bathroom with his towel over his shoulder, Pio saw a fellow novice, a very nervous soul who was afraid of his own shadow. The other novice did not notice Pio, who could not resist skulking behind a table, which had on it two candlesticks and a human skull.[4] As the nervous novice crept by the table, Pio groaned and flapped his towel at the boy, who, terrified, fled screaming.

"Wait, it's only me," Pio called, running to silence him before the novice master heard and they got in trouble. Being chased only made the boy scream louder. Finally, Pio caught up to him, just as the boy, in his terror, tripped and fell. Unable to stop in time, Pio tumbled atop the boy, who was so scared that he was too numb to even know where he was. Far from repentant over having so frightened someone, for the rest of his life Pio loved to tell this story.

Ordinary, yet Extraordinary

If the young Capuchin seminarian was down to earth in his good humor and his love of pranks, his extraordinary predilection for prayer soon showed his Franciscan spiritual directors that Pio was anything but ordinary in his spiritual life.

Padre Leone of San Giovanni Rotondo was the supervisor of studies at one of the friaries where Pio did part of his studies for the priesthood. Padre Leone says "I ... would often go to visit him in his cell and I almost always found him praying on his knees with his eyes red from crying. I could say that he was a student who prayed continually, and these prayers were made up of tears as it was enough to look at his eyes to understand that tears were habitual visitors." While the supervisor of studies confesses that he found Pio praying instead of studying, he witnesses, "However, in school he always knew the lesson in spite of the fact that we were of the opinion that he studied very little." Was this because Pio was an intellectual genius? Padre Leone does not think so, characterizing Pio as "of average intelligence." It is Pio's *spiritual* rather than intellectual genius that seems to account for his ability to master subjects more through prayer than study.

Tears, Tears, Tears

If Pio's spiritual genius was first hinted at by his exemplary behavior (he himself admitted he was never scolded even once as a novice), it was further confirmed in his gift of tears.

Not only Padre Leone saw that Pio wept a great deal when praying. Padre Damaso of S. Elia a Pianisi recalls, "One evening (this would be around 1904), we were praying silently in the choir.... Spurred on by devotion mixed with curiosity, I stealthily placed my finger on a large white handkerchief that Frater Pio had at his side, and I thought of the gift of tears (it was said that he had an eye problem as a result of the many tears he shed). I withdrew my finger, which was now completely soaked, as the handkerchief was drenched with tears. From that moment, something particular was conceived in my soul for Frater Pio's goodness."

Finally, Padre Antonio of San Giovanni Rotondo recalls Pio shed "enough tears to form a dent in the floor, during prayer time, and especially after Holy Communion. When asked the reason for those tears, the little Frater would always withdraw into himself and become silent. As his spiritual director, I finally obliged him to speak: '*I cry*,' he said, '*for my sins and those of mankind*.'"

A Prophecy

Sometime during those years of studies, Pio made an interesting prophecy to a fellow student, Romolo of San Marco in Lamis, who was just a year and a few days older than Pio. Handed a piece of paper, Romolo saw that Pio had written in Latin "*Romolo, statutum est te mori post me et mori senem,*" which in English means, "Romolo, it is established that you will die after I do and you will be very old." Many years later, Padre Romolo died on February 1, 1981, at the age of ninety-five. Although a year older than Pio, he had outlived him by thirteen years.

No Saint in the Making: Just a Good Little Friar

Frater Pio spent time over a period of several years at various Capuchin houses as he progressed through his studies toward priestly ordination. Everywhere he went, he was esteemed and loved, but no one thought of him as a saint—or even a saint in the making.

For instance, in 1907, Padre Agostino of San Marco in Lamis, who some years later would become Frater Pio's spiritual director, noted that Pio—who was then studying philosophy—was "good, obedient, studious, even if [as was already often the case] he was ailing." Still Padre Agostino did not see "anything extraordinary or supernatural in him." Pleasant and good-humored to others, during this time from age eighteen to twenty-one, Pio suffered horribly from scruples, worrying constantly that he was not pleasing to God.

Yet, even while suffering greatly both from poor health and scruples, hidden supernatural phenomena continued to be part of Pio's life. The best-known incident, revealed under obedience to Padre Agostino years later, was already two years past at the time Agostino took Pio for just a good little friar.

It had taken place on the night of January 18, 1905. As was his custom, at about eleven at night, rather than hitting the philosophy books, Pio was praying in the choir. He later wrote under obedience:

I suddenly found myself far away in an elegant house, where the father was dying while his child was being born. Then Most Holy Mary appeared to me and said: "I confide this creature to your care; it is a precious stone in the unpolished state. Work on it; polish it; make it as shiny as possible, because one day I want to adorn myself with it..."

"How will this be possible when I am still a poor student

and don't even know whether I will have the joy of becoming a priest? And even if I do become a priest, how will I be able to think of this baby girl, being so far away from here?"

The Madonna replied: "Do not doubt. It will be she who will come to you, but beforehand you will meet her in Saint Peter's...."

After this I found myself once more in the choir.

A hallucination? One could think so, but Pio's experience of somehow being in two places at the same time (a mystical phenomenon known as bilocation) was corroborated by Giovanna Rizzani, the child who was born that night. Her father did indeed die on the date given by Padre Pio, throwing her pregnant mother into premature labor and resulting in Giovanna's birth. Years later, in 1922, in Rome, the eighteen-year-old student, struggling with spiritual doubts, went to Saint Peter's and asked a Capuchin priest who came toward her to please hear her confession. They went into the confessional, and there the Capuchin resolved all her difficulties.

Although the church was closing, she hung around outside the confessional, wanting to express her joy and gratitude to this wonderful, unknown confessor. Finally told she would have to leave, and the Capuchin still not having exited his side of the confessional, she knocked and then peered inside. The confessional, under her scrutiny ever since she had exited, was empty.

In her summer 1923 holidays she visited San Giovanni Rotondo, where Padre Pio—who at that time had not physically left San Giovanni since 1918—greeted her with "I know you. You were born the night your father died." Amazed, she was even more astounded the following day when she entered the confessional of Padre Pio. "My daughter, at last you've come!" he said with enthusiasm. "I've waited many years for you."

"You must be confusing me with someone else. This is my first time here."

"No, I haven't mistaken you for some other girl. You already know me; you came to me last year in Saint Peter's Basilica." Then he told her more things, including the fact that she had been entrusted to his care upon her birth by the Madonna.

The poor girl was so shocked that she wondered aloud if all this meant she must become a nun.

"Nothing of the sort," he assured her.

Eventually his spiritual child married and became the Marchioness Boschi of Cesena, but she pursued a holy life under Pio's guidance. When she became a Third Order (lay) Franciscan, he named her Sister Jacoba. Those familiar with St. Francis of Assisi will recall the Lady Jacoba was one of Francis' closest friends.

Finally, there is corroboration from Giovanna's mother, Leonilde Rizzani. While her husband lay terminally ill, Leonilde—eight months pregnant with her sixth child—was praying fervently that her spouse, an ardent Mason who hated the church, would make peace with God. He adamantly declined to see a priest and his Mason friends surrounded the house so that if Leonilde summoned one, the priest would not gain entry.

As her husband slipped into a coma, Leonilde continued her prayers, kneeling at his bedside. Suddenly—at the same time Pio had his experience of being in the Rizanni house— she saw a young priest in a Capuchin habit. When she got up to follow him out of the room, he seemed to disappear in thin air. Before she could figure out what was going on, the family dog began to howl. In this part of Italy, a baying dog is said to be a harbinger of death. Upset, Leonilde thought to go out and untie the dog in the yard. Before she got to the door, she went into labor. She shouted, and the family business manager who was there helped her deliver a baby girl.

The business manager then went out, informed the Masons that a baby had been born prematurely and they had no business keeping a priest from coming in to baptize the child. For hours, a priest had been trying to get in the house. Permitted now, he rushed to the dying man's bedside. Rizzani opened his eyes and said distinctly, "My God! My God! Forgive me!" Then he lapsed back into a coma and died before morning.

Leonilde's experience of Pio's presence dovetails perfectly with what Pio says he witnessed in his written account to his superiors. The superiors kept the entire matter quiet, but in time his entire order and eventually the world would have many other witnesses of Padre Pio's bilocations.

His Mysterious Illness

God definitely toys with those He loves in games of spiritual hide-and-seek, or a kind of spiritual yo-yoing that is meant to make a soul utterly pliant in God's hands. In Padre Pio's case, times of ecstatic closeness—such as his vision before leaving his family to join the Capuchins—alternated with times when Jesus seemed far away and Pio suffered the pangs of unrequited love.

One way in which God yo-yoed with Pio was his health. From shortly after entering the Franciscans, Pio suffered mysterious bouts of illness. Part of this may have been due to his strenuous prayer life, which left him with literally no taste for food beyond the Eucharist. Yet even when he plumped up some and looked such a picture of health that he was affectionately dubbed *il piu bello* ("the most handsome"), Pio suffered intensely. He often could keep nothing down but milk for long periods. He also suffered terrible headaches and fevers so high that they broke regular thermometers, which are made to go no higher than 106 degrees. Using a bath thermometer, friars, and doctors they called in, recorded temperatures in Pio of 120 degrees. Yet he did not die or suffer brain damage.

The Fires of Love

Since they had none of the expected physiological effects, the record-setting temperatures were perhaps related somehow to the fact that Pio was one of the mystics who burn, even physically, with love for God. In his letters to his spiritual directors, he sometimes writes about this:

I feel my heart and my inmost being completely absorbed by the mounting flames of an immense fire. These flames cause my poor soul to give vent to pitiful laments. Yet who would believe it? While my soul experiences an atrocious agony caused by the flames I have described, it is filled at the same time by an exceeding sweetness which calls forth immense love of God.

The flames of divine love burned but did not consume Pio:

I feel myself annihilated, dear Father, and I cannot find anywhere to hide from this gift of the Divine Master. I am sick with an illness of the heart. I cannot go on any longer. The thread of life seems ready to break from one moment to the next, yet this moment never comes.

My dear Father, the soul is in a sad state when God has made it sick with His love.

Years later, when saying Mass, he recalled:

> *It seems to me at times that it* [my heart] *must burst out of my chest. Sometimes at the altar my whole body burns in an indescribable manner. My face, in particular, seems to go on fire.*

He felt unable to "*pour out this ever-active volcano which burns me up and which Jesus has placed in this very small heart. It can all be summed up as follows: I am consumed by love for God and love for my neighbor. God is constantly fixed in my mind and imprinted on my heart. I never lose sight of Him.*"

During His Student Years

Because of Pio's strange physical breakdowns in health, including the horrific fevers, the friars repeatedly had to send Pio home to Pietrelcina. There, each time, the good air, the simple food cooked by his mother, and the love of his family would restore him to some semblance of health—health which, unfortunately, vanished as soon as he returned to a friary.

In May 1909, he was sent home again. This time he would stay until February 1916, to the great unhappiness of his Superiors. No malingerer, Pio simply could not seem to live outside of Pietrelcina. As time went on and he continued to be unable to return to the friary, he suffered agonies that his Superiors would decide to expel him from the Order.

Family Ties

Giuseppa Forgione had nobly given her son to God and the Franciscan Order. Yet, she could not help but be happy when he returned to Pietrelcina. Convinced over the years that the Capuchin Franciscan way of life was just too austere for her beloved son, Mama Forgione pressed Pio to leave the Order and become a parish priest in his hometown. To Pio—whose deepest fear at this time was being ordered to leave his religious community—his mother's attitude was another burden.

During his years at home, Pio's older brother and father remained working in America, although they returned every few years for a visit. Among his three sisters, his favorite, Felicita, would marry a friend of Pio's; a second, Graziella, would move toward becoming a nun.

The third sister's story reminds us that even saints' prayers are not omnipotent, nor are their families perfect. The "family for whom God is everything," as neighbors called the Forgiones, had a black sheep. Pio's middle sister Pellegrina, in one of those mysteries of free will, seemed able to resist Pio's and her entire family's prayers, living a scandalous life and even characterized by some people as "a devil." In 1913, when Pio had been home about four years, Pellegrina became pregnant out of wedlock. Not long after she finally eased the scandal by marrying the father of her daughter, he deserted her and left for America. It is said that her second child, a boy, who died as a toddler during the 1918 flu epidemic, was also born out of wedlock. Pio—who would convert thousands of people in his lifetime—appeared to have failed with his own sister.

The Villagers

At first Pio did not have great success with the other locals, either. In a day when TB was a dreaded scourge, Pio was at first unwelcome in some homes because they feared he might carry the deadly infection to their children. Eventually it was realized that whatever his illness was, it was not contagious.

Many also tended to dismiss the young Capuchin as a fanatic and crank when his Mass frequently took over two hours while he went into ecstasy. Eventually, his goodness won them over (the parish priest also put Pio under obedience to shorten the Mass). Over time, the word began to circulate that Pio was a saint and the man to see if you needed special prayers for something.

Of Priest and Angel

Padre Pio found a great support in the local parish priest Don Salvatore Pannullo, a former seminary and college professor, called *Zi' Tore*, "Uncle Tore," by the locals and *Pati*, "Little Father," by Pio. Pio assisted this priest—whose altar boy he had once been—with parish duties and turned to him for priestly friendship and counsel (in addition to that he received by mail from his Franciscan spiritual directors, Padre Benedetto and Padre Agostino).

It is Don Salvatore Pannullo, an intelligent, well-qualified witness, who documented unusual things that Pio, living as quietly as possible, would have simply never made known. For instance, one day Pio received a letter in Greek (a language Pio didn't know) from Padre Agostino, who didn't want the letter to be read by just anyone. Yet Pio read the Greek readily and explained the letter to Don Salvatore.

"How can you read this?" the local priest asked.

"My guardian angel explained it all to me," Pio replied.

Another time the same thing happened with a letter that had been sent in French.

Padre Pio, Priest and Victim

On July 1, 1910, the Father Provincial of the Capuchin Franciscans gave Padre Pio, who had continued his studies in Pietrelcina, the needed dispensation and set the date for Pio's priestly ordination. Padre Benedetto, both as Father Provincial and as one of Padre Pio's two spiritual directors, assured Pio that the enemy, wanting to keep Pio upset, had insinuated Pio's fears that he was sinning. Jesus, Benedetto told the young Capuchin, "is very pleased with your soul, which he intends to purify and adorn by means of many trials."

On July 30, 1910, accompanied by his parish priest and friend, Don Salvatore Pannullo, Pio traveled to Benevento to take his exams. He passed, and on August 10 Frater Pio became Padre Pio when he was ordained in the Cathedral of Benevento. His mother and other relatives were there, but his father and only brother were in America. When the family returned to Pietrelcina, Pio's brother's wife had hired a brass band to greet them, while villagers presented the new priest with coins and gifts.

First Mass

On August 14, Pio sang his first solemn High Mass in his hometown. That day he wrote: *"Jesus, my breath, my life. Today, with trembling hands, I elevate you in a mystery of*

Divine Love. May I, with you, be for the world, the way, the truth, and the life, and for you a holy priest, a perfect victim."

When August 14 came round each year, Padre Pio's heart never failed to spill over with gratitude; time and again he would feel his heart *"inflamed* [more] *than ever with love for Jesus,"* who had let him become a priest.

Saying Mass would always be the highlight of Padre Pio's day—and indeed his life. Afire with divine love, Pio seemed to merge with the Christ he called down from heaven with the words "this is my body; this is my blood." When Pio received the consecrated wafer that Catholics, following Scripture, believe is truly Christ's Body and Blood, he tasted *"the sweetness of that Immaculate Flesh of the Son of God."* In fact, so many consolations did Pio receive saying Mass, he admitted that if he could only bury the consolations in his heart, the organ would become Paradise.

How happy Jesus makes me! How sweet is His spirit! But I am confused and can do nothing but weep and repeat: "Jesus, my food!..." What distresses me most is that I repay all this love of Jesus with so much ingratitude.... He continues to love me and to draw me closer to Himself. He has forgotten my sins and I would say that He remembers only His own mercy.... Each morning He comes into my heart and pours out all the effusions of His goodness.

Surrender

Seeing himself as ungrateful, and continuing to struggle after his ordination with illness and diabolical persecution, Pio still steadfastly trusted in God. "*Let the most holy and most lovable will of God be done in me and all around me; at all times and in all things! This is what ... enable[s] me to carry on.... I know that He never acts except for most holy ends which are for our good.*"

Strange Happenings

It is Don Pannullo to whom the young priest ran on September 7, 1910, showing Pati the deep puncture wounds that had appeared in Pio's hands while he was praying. Pio said he received them when Jesus and Mary appeared to him.

Don Pannullo insisted Pio consult a doctor. The first doctor diagnosed "tubercular lesions." The second scoffed "Absolutely not!" but admitted he did not know what had caused the wounds. A few days after seeing the second doctor, a deeply embarrassed Padre Pio asked Pati to pray with him to ask Jesus to take away the wounds, adding that he was *"glad to suffer, even to die of suffering"* to help bring about the Kingdom of God—as long as it was *"all in secret."*

Pati prayed with Pio, reminding him to say to Jesus "Do with me as Thou will," and the wounds—which only the two doctors, the priest, and one of Pio's good friends had seen—went away. But a year later, in September 1911, Pio still had pain in his palms and red marks there.

In 1912 Padre Pio wrote Padre Agostino. *"From Thursday evening up to Saturday and on Tuesday also, a painful tragedy takes place. My heart, hands and feet seem to be pierced through by a sword, so great is the pain I feel."*

His Other Mother

As an aged man on his deathbed, Padre Pio would say, "I see two mothers." From boyhood he had seen visions of the Virgin Mary, and his love for her, like his love for his earthly mother was profound. The Capuchins point out that his love for the Mother of God came from his meditations on Mary's role in the plan of salvation, a role devised by God.

Pio himself spoke of being *"held fast and bound to the Son by means of this mother"* in a letter to his spiritual directors, for it was God's will that, as Pio explained:

This most tender mother in her great mercy, wisdom and goodness, has been pleased to punish me in a most exalted manner, by pouring so many and such great graces into my heart that when I am in her presence, and in that of Jesus, I am compelled to exclaim: "Where am I? ... Who is this who is near me? I am all aflame although there is no fire."

And he wrote again to his directors, *"I wish I had a voice strong enough to invite the sinners of the world to love Our Lady."*

Padre Pio on the Rosary

Love our Lady and make her loved; always recite the rosary and recite it as often as possible. [To comments that the rosary had had its day] *Let's do what we have always done; that which our fathers always did and we will be fine.... Satan always tries to destroy this prayer, but he will never succeed. It is the prayer of He who triumphs over all and everyone. And she has taught us this prayer just as Jesus taught us the Our Father.*

When someone asked whether one should pay attention to the words of the Hail Mary, (i.e., vocal prayer or to the mental contemplation of the mysteries of the rosary), he replied:

The attention must be on the "Hail Mary" and to the greetings which you give to the Virgin and on the mysteries which you contemplate. She is present in all the mysteries and she participated in everything with love and pain.

In Padre Pio's letter dated May 13, 1915, to the Franciscan tertiary Raffaelina Cerase:

Reflect upon and keep before your mental gaze the great humility of the Mother of God, our Mother. The more she was filled with heavenly gifts, the more deeply did she humble herself, so that she was able to say when overshadowed by the Holy Spirit, who made her the Mother of God's Son, "Behold the Handmaid of the Lord." This dear Mother of ours was to break forth with the same words in the home of St. Elizabeth, although she bore in her chaste womb the Word Incarnate.

Seven Years of Purification

While Pio felt God put him in Pietrelcina at this time to help certain souls, he was also there for his own spiritual growth. A time of purification, his years in Pietrelcina were given in large part to prayer, during which he experienced ecstasies and joy. But much of his time after 1915 was spent in what theologians call "the dark night," a kind of passive cleansing of the soul through spiritual darkness and aridity in prayer. This would reach its zenith around 1918 but not end there.

It has been said by those who lived with Padre Pio, as well as those who conducted the formal investigation of his life before his beatification, that from at least 1915 he remained always in a kind of spiritual dark night. Able to see the condition of other souls clearly, he had no idea whether his own soul was pleasing to the Lord. Living in close union with

God, even while he obtained great miracles for others through his prayers, Pio remained in a kind of fog about his own spiritual situation so that he never presumed his own salvation. It seems that God could maintain Pio in his great humility, while pouring out on him so many spiritual charisms and graces, only by blinding him to his own spiritual greatness.

In Pietrelcina even as people were beginning to speak of him as a saint, in 1914 Pio wrote his spiritual director: "*I see myself so deformed that it seems as if my very clothing shrinks in horror of my defilement.*" And in 1915 he wrote his director that the thought that he *might* sin, "*fills me with terror. It paralyzes my limbs and both body and soul feel as if they are being squeezed in a powerful vise. My bones feel as if they were being ... crushed.*" At that time he found himself in "*an endless desert of darkness ... a land of death, a night of abandonment ... in which my poor soul finds itself far from God and alone.*"

That Pio was separated at this time by reason of his health from the Franciscans has resulted in the treasure of his letters to Padre Benedetto and Padre Agostino, his spiritual directors. These letters provide invaluable insight into Pio's resolve "*to love God or die.*"

Dealing With His Visions

During his years at home, from time to time Pio would report under orders to a friary to try to live in community. He always immediately became so sick that he was soon sent back to Pietrelcina. But during one six-week stay in 1911, his directors discovered some of the supernatural phenomena that Pio would never voluntarily discuss even with them.

Confined to bed most of the time and able to retain in his stomach only the Eucharist, Pio was observed by Padre Agostino of San Marco in Lamis who thought him "deliriously ill." The Padre wrote in his diary:

Nobody was aware of any supernatural phenomena, not even I. I thought he was really ill and furthermore, in danger of death. I went to his room where there were some other friars also, and I saw Padre Pio lying on the bed with an agitated expression on his face and he said: "Send away that cat which wants to fling itself on me."

I couldn't endure that scene so I went to the choir to pray for Padre Pio, fearing that he would die. After more than fifteen minutes I returned to the room and found a serene and cheerful Padre Pio, alone. As soon as he saw me, he said: *"You did the right thing going to the choir to pray ... You even thought about my funeral eulogy ... There's still time, Padre, there's time."*

Only then did Padre Agostino, who had been one of Pio's two directors for some time, realize that Pio had been having a diabolical vision. The devil, in those years, appeared to Pio in various forms: as his guardian angel, St. Francis, Our Lady, even Padre Agostino. Other times the devil appeared in the form of a crucifix, nude young women, torturers who whipped Pio and, finally, as Satan himself surrounded by dark spirits.

Gradually his directors uncovered that Pio also had ecstatic visions of Jesus, of Mary, and other mystical phenomena. Visions of Jesus were proved genuine, his directors believed, by the great benefits they left in Pio's soul. But they were aware—as was Pio—of how many souls have gone astray because they insisted, out of pride, on relying on what they were told in visions.

Telling Padre Benedetto about something Pio learned from Jesus through a vision, Pio wrote, "*Examine this present letter, please, and if you should find in it any deception of the devil, then do not spare me in undeceiving me. This thought makes me tremble, for I do not want to be a victim of the devil.*"

With the wisdom of true humility, Pio would never give any vision or locution[5] confidence until it had been reported to and approved by his spiritual directors. Another time, on this subject, he wrote Padre Benedetto: "*As you know, Padre, I would not wish to be a victim of the devil in anything whatsoever, and although I am more certain of the reality of those locutions than I am of my own existence, I am still struggling against myself and protest that I want to believe nothing of all this, for the sole reason that you, my Directors, have cast a doubt upon it. Am I right or wrong in this?"* The young friar was assured he was right, that God would prefer he humbly assent to his directors' counsel than that he serve ego by following visions—which can have many sources besides God.

Bringing Souls to God

In constant touch with his spiritual directors by letter, at this time Pio repeatedly begged their permission to offer himself as a victim for poor sinners and the souls in purgatory. In one of those mysteries of sanctity, at the very time that Jesus accepted Pio's offering and the young Capuchin's physical and other sufferings increased, Pio also had moments where he experienced "indescribable joy."

It was during these years in Pietrelcina that Pio began giving his own spiritual direction by letter to those trying to find or come closer to God. In the hundreds of letters he wrote over the next few years, Pio carefully addressed only spiritual matters, avoiding his correspondents' worldly concerns except where these had a spiritual dimension. These letters reveal Pio as a man steeped in the Scriptures, totally dedicated to Jesus Christ, and exquisitely sensitive to the subtlest spiritual currents of the soul.

An example of Pio's human and supernatural sensitivity is the following letter to Padre Agostino, who has asked guidance for a pair of wealthy aristocrats—without telling his spiritual son anything of the pair's high social standing or wealth. In his counsel, written in August 1913, the young Pio reveals complete understanding of how readily good people can fall into that self-righteousness Pio calls by the old-fashioned term vainglory:

Jesus wants me to speak of vainglory so as to put them on their guard against such a powerful enemy. This is an enemy that assails those who have consecrated themselves to the Lord and embraced the spiritual life. Hence it can rightly be called the consuming moth of souls tending to perfection. The Saints refer to it as the woodworm of holiness.

In order that we might understand how opposed vainglory is to perfection, Our Lord shows how he reprimanded the Apostles when he found them full of complacency and vainglory because the devils had obeyed their command ... It seeps into the holiest acts and even into humility itself, and if one is not watchful, it proudly sets up its tent.... The devil ... knows very well that a man who is lustful, greedy, or avaricious, a sinner, has more reason to be confused and to blush than to glory in his actions and therefore he takes care not to tempt him on this score, but if he spares such persons from this battle, he does not spare good people, especially those who are striving for perfection. All the other vices hold sway only over those who allow themselves to be vanquished and mastered by them, but vainglory raises its head against those very persons who combat and defeat it. It is an enemy that is never wearied....

St. Jerome was quite right when he compared vainglory to one's shadow. In point of fact, our shadow follows us everywhere...; if we run, it runs too. If we proceed at a slow pace, the shadow does likewise.... Vainglory acts in the same way: it follows virtue everywhere.... Once it gets in [to the soul] it mars every virtue, corrodes all holiness and corrupts everything that is beautiful and good.

They should strive to ask God constantly for the grace to be preserved from this pestilential vice.... Let them open wide their hearts to trust in God, always bearing in mind that all that is good in them is a pure gift of the Heavenly Bridegroom's supreme bounty.

They should impress on their minds, engrave deeply in their hearts and be convinced that no one is good except God and that all we have is nothing. They must continue to meditate assiduously on what St. Paul wrote the faithful of Corinth: "What have you that you did not receive? If then you received it, why do you boast as if it were not a gift?" (1 Cor 4:7). "Not that we are sufficient of ourselves," he writes elsewhere, "to claim anything as coming from us; our sufficiency is from God" (2 Cor 3:5).

When these two people feel tempted to vainglory they should repeat with St. Bernard, "I haven't begun for you [i.e., to feel self-righteous], nor do I want to finish for you...." If the enemy attacks them on the score of the holiness of their lives, let them shout in his face: "My holiness is not an effect of my own spirit, but it is the Spirit of God who sanctifieth me. This is a gift from God. It is a talent lent to me by my Spouse so that I can trade with it and when the time comes give Him an exact account of the profit I have gained." They should conceal the good their Beloved is operating in them. The virtues are to be kept as a person keeps a treasure which, if not hidden from the sight of envious people, will be seized. The devil is always on the watch; he is the most envious of all and he seeks to seize at once this treasure consisting of the virtues as soon as he recognizes it. This he does by having us attacked by this powerful enemy which is vainglory.

In order to preserve us from this great adversary, Our Lord, who is always concerned for our good, warns us on this point in various parts of the Gospel.

Let them invariably direct their actions to the pure glory of God as the Apostle wishes: "So whether you eat or drink or whatever you do, do all to the glory of God" (1 Cor 10:31). They should renew this holy intention every now and then. They should examine themselves after each action and if they recognize any imperfection in it, they should not

*be upset but repent and humble themselves before the good-
ness of God, ask pardon of the Lord and implore him to
make them more careful in future.*

*They must avoid all vanity in dress for the Lord allows
souls to fall because of such vanity. A woman who is frivo-
lous as regards dress ... loses all adornment of soul once this
idol enters into her heart.*

Pio ends by recommending the avoidance of "costly attire
which is a sign of luxury and ostentation."

Discerning on Fear of Salvation

While the counsel of his two older spiritual directors
remained absolutely necessary for Pio as he walked in darkness regarding his own soul, by 1913, as the above letter
demonstrates, Padres Benedetto and Agostino were also turn-
ing to the young friar for his advice. Knowing that Padre
Benedetto of San Marco in Lamis was "perplexed in mind,"
Pio wrote the following comforting words to him:

*Our Lord appeared and spoke to me as follows: "My son, do
not fail to write down what you hear today from my lips, so that
you may not forget it. I am faithful and no creature will be lost
unwittingly. Light is very different from darkness. I invariably*

attract to myself a soul to whom I am accustomed to speak. On the contrary, the wiles of the devil tend to separate it from me. I never inspire in the soul any fears that drive it away from me; the devil never places in the soul any fears that induce it to draw near me. If the fears which the soul feels at certain moments of its life on the score of eternal salvation proceed from me, they can be recognized by the peace and serenity they leave in the soul."

Raffaelina Cerase

Among the first people to whom Padre Pio gave extensive spiritual guidance by mail was Raffaelina Cerase, one of the two aristocratic sisters whom Padre Agostino first introduced to Pio by letter. Raffaelina Cerase lived with her older sister in the southern Italian city of Foggia. Her letters to Pio and his replies fill an entire volume of his writings.

In a letter to Raffaelina Cerase, May 19, 1914, Padre Pio writes:

Beloved daughter in Jesus Christ,

May Jesus and Mary be always in your heart and may they make you holy.

By repeated blows of the efficacious chisel and by diligent polishing the divine Artist prepares the blocks of stone which are intended to form part of the divine edifice. Thus sings our most tender Mother the holy Catholic church in the hymn of the Office for the Dedication of a Church, and this is very true.

Every soul intended for eternal glory can very well be considered a stone destined for the erection of the eternal edifice.

The soul that is destined to reign with Jesus Christ in eternal glory, then, must be remodeled by the blows of hammer and chisel. But what are these blows ... by which the divine Artist prepares the stone, that is to say, the chosen soul? Dear sister, these strokes of the chisel are the shadows, fears, temptations, spiritual torments and agitation, with a dash of desolation and even of physical pain.

Thank the infinite mercy of the eternal Father, then, for treating your soul in this way, for it is destined to be saved. What I say is, why not rejoice at this loving treatment by the best of all fathers? Open your heart to this heavenly Physician of souls and abandon yourself with complete confidence in His most holy embrace. He is treating you as one chosen to follow Jesus closely up the Hill of Calvary and I observe with joy and keenest emotion this action of grace in you. Be quite sure that all that is going on within your soul is decreed by the Lord and for this reason you must not be afraid of acting wrongly, in a word, of offending God.

Let it suffice for you to know that in all this ... on the contrary, He is glorified all the more.... If this most tender

❖

Spouse hides from your soul, it is not because He intends to punish your infidelity, as you imagine, but because He wants to test more and more your faith and steadfastness and at the same time to purify you of certain little attachments which to the eyes of the flesh do not appear as such. I am speaking here of those affections and faults from which not even the righteous are exempt, for it is written in the holy pages that a righteous man falls seven times [a day, see Prv 24:16].

Believe me, if I did not see you so disconsolate, I should be less satisfied, for I should see the Lord bestowing less jewels on you. Hold firm, then, and banish as temptations all doubts on the subject, for they are really temptations. Do this in the name of Jesus on whose behalf I tell you that in all these spiritual combats you are not offending God, you are not committing sin and your soul derives much profit from it all.

Once more, get rid of all those doubts which are clouding the heavens of your soul, such as the idea that you are deaf to the divine call, that you resist his tender invitations, that you yourself are the only obstacle in the way of perfection on the part of your sister, for this does not come from the good spirit but consists in the devil's cunning attempts to turn you aside from your purpose, or at least to make you pause in your progress towards perfection and lose heart.

I hope I have said enough on the subject and that you

will heed what I say. I urge you to pray continually to the heavenly Father that He may always keep you close to His divine Heart, [so] that He may make you hear His loving voice more and more clearly and lead you to correspond with increasing gratitude. Ask Jesus with boundless confidence, like the bride in the Song of Solomon, to draw you after Him and let you smell the fragrance of his anointing oils [see Sg 1:3-4] so that you may follow swiftly with all the faculties of your soul and body wherever He goes [Revelation 14:4].

If Jesus manifests Himself, thank Him and if He remains hidden, thank Him just the same: all is a trick of love. I earnestly hope that you will come to breathe your last with Jesus on the Cross and with Him softly exclaim: It is finished.

Your desire to feel the Creator alone in all things and the tedium you experience in approaching and dealing with creatures is a most singular grace of the divine mercy which is not granted to all poor wayfarers. Make sure, then, that you know how to profit by it and thank God for it. Don't listen to what your imagination tells you, for it is upset and powerfully attacked by our enemy, who wants you to consider your life unproductive of good. This is merely a clever plot contrived by the devil. The grace of Jesus, my dear, makes you only too watchful with regard to what is good. You are trying to measure, understand, feel and touch this love which you have for God, but, my dear sister, you must accept as certain that the more a soul loves God the less it feels this love.

The thing seems too strange and impossible in the case of transient love for creatures in this poor world, but when it is a case of love for the Spouse of the soul, things are very different. I am not able to explain this truth very clearly, but you can take it as certain that the matter is as I have said. God is incomprehensible and inaccessible; hence the more a soul penetrates into the love of this Supreme Good, the more the sentiment of love toward Him, which is beyond the soul's knowledge, seems to diminish, until the poor soul considers that it no longer loves Him at all.

In point of fact, in certain instances it seems to the soul that this is really the case, but the events prove the very opposite. That continual fear of losing one's God, that holy circumspection which makes one look carefully where to place one's feet so as not to stumble, that courage in facing the assaults of the enemy, that resignation to God's will in all life's adversities, that ardent desire to see God's kingdom established in one's own heart and in the hearts of others, are the clearest proof of the soul's love for the Supreme Good.

No, your love is not indolent, nor is it sterile. You ought rather to say that you love your heavenly Bridegroom, but that you want that love to grow continually.

The divine Master has left us in writing the injunction

to recognize as our brethren those only who do the will of His Father [see Mtt 12:50]. *Well, then, do you not desire and make every effort to conform at all times to the divine will? Would you not give your life a thousand times rather than resolve to go against God's will? You are quite sure of this and you feel it in your heart. Let this, then, be the touchstone by which you recognize and convince yourself that your life is well spent.*

Oh, how far you are from that which your feelings would lead you to believe! You love this most tender Spouse, but this seems very little to you because you desire to love with a perfect and consummate love. To us wretched and unfortunate mortals this love, at least in its fullness, is only granted in the next life. O wretched condition of our human nature! May our heavenly Spouse break through this thinnest of thin veils which separates us from Him and grant us at last that perfect love....

A Holy—and Fruitful—Death

In February 1916, Raffaelina was dying of breast cancer that had spread after a mastectomy. She had been perfectly well while her older sister was near death from liver disease, until Raffaelina offered God her life for her sister's health and for Padre Pio's ability to live in a friary without terrible illnesses.

After that prayer, her sister got well and lived another fifteen years.

Raffaelina asked Pio's Franciscan Superiors if he could come assist her on her deathbed. They assented and Padre Pio took the train from Pietrelcina to Foggia, intending to remain only a few days. Unknown to Pio, however, Raffaelina had also urged Pio's two spiritual directors to order him to remain in the friary. She also said they should give him permission to hear confessions [he had been thought too young and unseasoned a priest for this work]. "He will save many souls," she predicted of his future work in the confessional.

In Foggia, Pio said Mass daily in the private chapel of the saintly aristocrat, heard her final confession, and assisted her at her holy death. Not long after, she appeared to him in heavenly glory, making Pio, who longed to die and be with God, long even more for death.

But his request to his spiritual directors for permission to die[6] received a flat "no." Then, emboldened by Raffaelina's prophecies, Padre Benedetto ordered Pio, "Dead or alive, you're staying in Foggia!"

Obediently, Pio wrote his mother and Don Pannullo and prepared to stay. The climate, especially as the year moved into summer's heat, did not agree with Padre Pio. Struggling to breathe through that summer, Pio was sent in September to a remote friary high above Foggia in the Gargano Mountains. There it was cooler and the air better suited to him. Raffaelina had not offered her life in vain: except for a few weeks in the military Pio would remain in this Our Lady of Grace Friary the rest of his life.

World War I

During his years at home, struggles between various world powers culminated in the outbreak of World War I in 1914. Italy was swept into the conflict, and the Capuchins, an Order primarily of young men at that time, had many friars and seminarians called up. Pio received his notice—addressed to his birth name of Francesco Forgione—at the end of 1916, about ten months after Raffaelina Cerase's death. He was just one of some sixty Capuchins summoned.

His ill health now proved to have a positive side. After less than two weeks in a Naples army barracks, an army doctor found Private Forgione too ill to serve. On January 3, 1917, he was given six month's convalescent leave. Pio went back to his mountaintop friary with a detour to Pietrelcina to visit his loved ones.

He was called back to service in 1917, shortly after he had accompanied his sister Graziella to Rome where she entered the Briggitine Order. Pio, once again Private Forgione, remained in Naples from August to November, when he was again given convalescent leave, this time for four months. He returned to the military early in March 1918. By the middle of the month he was declared permanently unfit and discharged.

Such a great ascetic would be expected to shudder at joining the army. Pio *was* distressed but, typically, he worried even more about some of the other friars who had to do military service. Although sad to lay aside his beloved habit, he remained cheerful. He liked Naples and later recalled that during his brief military career there he met many nice people who treated him well.

An Account by Private Forgione, Padre Pio

In December of 1916, I was at the military hospital in Naples for observation. I was given a health leave. I was summoned to the captain's office ... where I was handed my papers and a free ticket from Naples to Benevento. I was also given one lira as a traveling allowance.

Leaving the hospital, I slowly made my way to the train station, passing through a piazza where there was a market. You've never seen anything if you haven't seen the markets in Naples, packed with happy people who are whistling and singing, who come and go in a never-ending state of chaos.

Out of curiosity, but also for a little distraction, I stopped for a while to see what people were selling. Then, as I was heading down the street to the train station, a man approached me who was selling paper umbrellas. He wanted one lira for them but said he would take fifty cents. Immediately I thought: "Since I'm going home, I'd really like to take something for my little nieces and nephews. Each of them would like something." I decided to buy them some souvenirs, but I knew that I only had one lira. "If I spend it," I said to myself, "what will I do to get to Pietrelcina?"

... At the Piazza Garibaldi ... more vendors were selling everything under the sun. I arrived at the station and went to the ticket window so that they could endorse my ticket. While I was walking to the tracks ... another man who was selling umbrellas approached me, saying, "Get your umbrellas now. See how beautiful they are? Hurry so you can get something for your children!"

I didn't pay attention to him, but he continued walking at my side, treating me first like I was a corporal then like I was a captain, when in fact I was only a simple soldier. Seeing how excited the man was ... I turned to him and said, "I don't want anything. I have no use for them. Anyway you're asking for a lira and a half while at the other market they were offering them for half a lira!" Since he was as stubborn as all the other street vendors, he said, "I have children. Help me out and buy some umbrellas." Handing me one, he said, "Out of love, take one as a souvenir for your loved ones." Still confronted with his banter, I asked, "You'll give it to me, then, for fifty cents?"

At that moment the whistle blew for the train to depart. I ran on board and looked out the window at that poor man who had wasted so much time and effort trying to sell me an umbrella so that he could take some bread home to his kids. I took fifty cents from my pocket and cried out: "Here, take this. May the Lord bless you." He was all excited and waved good-bye as the train left.

I was tired and burning up with a fever. I felt cold and wrapped my cape around me. The train got into Benevento rather late. As soon as I got off, I ran outside to catch a bus, but the bus to Pietrelcina had already left. So I had to spend the night in Benevento. I decided I'd stay in the train station so as not to bother my friends in Benevento.

I went back into the station and looked for a seat ... but it was packed with people. At the same time, my fever was going up and I could hardly stand anymore. When I got tired of sitting, I would walk around the station, both inside and out. The cold and the dampness penetrated my bones. I put up with these conditions for several hours. Often I was tempted to go into the coffee shop in the station since it was heated, but I was disappointed when I saw that it was filled with other soldiers and officers who were waiting for trains, and everyone was spending something for drinks.

I thought to myself "I only have fifty cents on me and if

I go in, what will I do?" I was feeling colder and colder all the time... still burning up with fever. It was two o'clock in the morning and there still wasn't an inch of space in the waiting room where I could lie down on the ground. I offered up the whole thing to the Lord and to my heavenly Mother. Finally I couldn't stand it anymore and went into the coffee shop. All the tables were taken. But I waited for someone to leave so that I could sit down for awhile. But no one got up.

Around half past three, they announced that the train for Foggia and Naples was leaving. Finally a couple of tables were free, but because of my timidity, I didn't make it in time to get a seat. I thought, "Even if I sit down, I don't have enough money to spend on a coffee. And if I don't buy anything, what will the poor owner earn after sacrificing his whole night here?" Finally, when it was four o'clock, more trains arrived and, thanks be to God, two tables were free in a corner of the coffee shop.

I sat down in the corner, hoping that the waiter wouldn't notice me. I had only sat down for a few minutes when three officers sat at the table next to me. Right away the waiter came and took their order. Then he asked me what I wanted. I, too, felt obliged to order a coffee. He served all four of us at the same time. The officers paid right away and left. I kept thinking, "If I drink it right away, I'll have to pay and go." But that coffee had to last me until the bus *arrived. Every time the waiter wasn't looking, I would sit still. When he would look at me, I'd take my spoon and pretend I was stirring some sugar in my coffee.*

Finally, the time came for the bus to arrive. I got up. I also got up the courage to pay. In a kind voice the waiter told me, "Thank you, soldier, but everything's been paid for." Since the waiter was quite elderly, I thought, "Maybe he knows me and wants to be nice to me." Also the thought crossed my mind that maybe the officers paid for me.

In any case, I thanked the waiter and went outside the station. I found the ... bus to Pietrelcina ... I looked around for someone I knew who might lend me the money for the ticket from Benevento to Pietrelcina, but in vain. The ticket cost a lira and eighty cents. "How will I pay with my fifty cents?" I asked myself.

Trusting in God, I got into the bus and sat down in the back so that I could talk with the ticket man and arrange to pay for the ticket when we arrived in Pietrelcina. At that moment, some other people got on. A very tall and handsome man sat down next to me. He had a new suitcase with him and set it on his knees. The bus was full, but I didn't see anyone I knew. I was afraid of embarrassing myself but I thought to myself, "Perhaps a lot of soldiers find themselves in my situation or worse. At least I have fifty cents." The bus left and the ticket man was taking the tickets of those people in the front of the bus. Slowly he made his way to me. The man next to me took a thermos and a cup out of his suitcase, and poured himself some hot coffee. Then he refilled the cup and offered me some ... I thanked him and tried to refuse ... but he insisted.... At that moment the ticket man came up and asked us where we were going.

I didn't even have a chance to open my mouth when he said to me, "Soldier, your ticket to Pietrelcina has been paid for." He handed me a ticket. On one hand, I was thrilled. But on the other hand I was mortified. "Who paid for it?" I asked myself. I wanted to know so I could thank that person at least. I asked God to bless that person for his good deed. Finally we got to Pietrelcina.... The man who sat next to me got off.... I followed him off the bus and turned around to say farewell and thank him. But I didn't see him again. He disappeared as if by magic. I looked around in every direction as I walked home, but I never saw him again.

Tinkling Bells of Sheep and Goats

In September 1916, when Padre Pio first took up residence miles above Foggia at the remote Capuchin friary of Our Lady of Grace in the mountains of the Gargano range, World War I was at its height. There were only a handful of friars at this friary, men who had escaped conscription for reasons of age or health. With them were seminarians too young to have been called up. These youngsters were being schooled in Franciscan tradition and Christian formation at this place so remote from worldly distractions.

A short ways down the hill there was a village called San Giovanni Rotondo but the villagers had their parish church, and few of them came up to the friary. As one friar who lived there remarked, about the only sound was the tinkling bells of the herds of sheep and goats pastured nearby. With its good cool mountain air, its solitude, and the devout atmosphere in which a handful of dedicated friars lived in brotherly love, Our Lady of Grace was an ideal place for Pio to hide himself in God.

Many thought Pio was preparing for death, for it was widely believed that the young priest would die soon from his serious lung and gastric ailments. Having been refused permission to die by his directors, however, Pio immediately turned his thoughts and energies back to saving souls. He loved spiritually shaping the seminarians, and he soon also had a group of local young women who came twice a week as a group for talks on the spiritual life. They began attending his morning Mass and making him their confessor as he led them toward sanctity.

Some of Padre Pio's "spiritual daughters" would become very holy women. However, in the beginning they were far from saints. In their humanity, most of them watched jealously to see how much time Pio gave the others in personal spiritual direction. Some complained when they saw that not all were receiving the same number of minutes.

Patiently, Padre Pio explained more than once that souls differ: some souls need only a quick, reassuring pat on the back while others need a complete work-over. To mollify his spiritual daughters, Pio told them: "*Some go to Paradise by train; others in a carriage and others on foot. The latter, however, have more merit and will have a place of greater glory in Paradise.*" And he replied to those who grumbled that he treated some sweetly and others sternly, "*You should realize that I do not act according to my humor, but according to God's will.*"

Like all parents trying to do right by children of varying temperaments and abilities, Pio found plenty of suffering in his spiritual children. One daughter says, "He alone knew how to administer [the right kind of mortification].... He beat the inside of the souls, and made the mire and all the good and bad passions come to the surface; the good, in order to exercise them and the bad, in order to uproot them."

It was not easy following a saint, they sometimes grumbled. But they knew that the prayer and sacrifices he offered God for their spiritual ascent were many times greater than anything he asked them to do.

Still Tending the Flock by Letters

During these first years at Our Lady of Grace, Padre Pio also continued to direct many souls by letter. On September 8, 1916, he writes Maria Gargani, a schoolteacher and active laywoman:

Most Beloved Daughter of the Heavenly Father, What will we give to the Lord in return for what He gives us?... We can still repeat with the prophet David. May Jesus be thanked, loved and blessed by heaven and earth. And may this most sweet God of ours always smile on your heart, my excellent daughter; may He always sustain your spirit, fill you with all his charisms and, lastly, reward you with eternal possession of him for the sacrifices you make and will make in the future for love of Him.

Your last letter does no less than move me, on considering the Lord's behavior for the good of your soul. I cannot but admire and bless our Heavenly Father for such exquisite behavior of His divine love towards you. How can one not rejoice at the sight of so many trials, to which the good Lord is subjecting you? Isn't the Cross certain and infallible proof of God's great love for a soul?

My daughter, I could not be pleased with you if I did not see you so tested. So take heart, bless the hand that afflicts you for the sole purpose of sanctifying you and rendering you similar to his only begotten Son. Don't believe that the Lord is irritated with you and therefore subjects you to such harsh trials. You would be greatly mistaken in this. The Lord wants to test your fidelity; he wants to inebriate you with the cross of his Son; he wants to purify you; he wants to increase your palm and crown.

Remember and keep well impressed in your mind that Calvary is the hill of the saints, but remember also that, after having climbed Calvary, the cross having been erected and you having died on it, you immediately ascend another mount, called Tabor, the heavenly Jerusalem. Remember that the suffering is short-lived but the reward is eternal.... The little ship of your spirit will never be submerged. Heaven and earth will pass away but the word of God assuring us that whoever obeys will sing victory [see Prv 21:28] will never pass away....

As regards your usual behavior in church, do not fear. The most useful, fruitful and also the most acceptable way to the Lord is precisely that: to ask Jesus to make us holy is neither presumption nor audacity, because it is the same as desiring to love Him greatly. The fears which arise as a result of your considering whether you spent your time [in Church] ... well or otherwise are without foundation. And dwelling on this is a true waste of time which could be used for ... more fruitful matters.

From a Letter to Maria Gargani
December 1917

Do you know what religion is? It is the academy of perfection in which each soul must learn to allow itself to be handled, planed, and smoothed by the divine Spirit,... so that ...[one] can be united and joined to the will of God.

The evident sign of perfection is that of being submitted to divine will in the trials of the spirit. Religion is a hospital for the spiritually ill who wish to be cured, and in order to achieve this they submit themselves to bleeding, the lancet, the razor, some probing, surgical instruments, fire and all the pains of medicine.

O my daughter, do not give too much importance to what the enemy and your imagination suggest to you regarding your interior suffering and spiritual aridity, being sure that this is best for you. Lovingly, sweetly, and lovably make this resolution: either to die or be cured. And as you don't want to die spiritually, try to be healed perfectly. And in order to be healed, desire to bear the treatment and correction of the divine doctor, and beseech Him not to spare you in anything in order to save you.

From Hundreds of Letters

Pio even wrote letters to people who lived just below the friary in the village of San Giovanni Rotondo. In a 1917 letter to a family there named Ventrella with whom he was friends, he encouraged three sisters:

Tell me once again, my dear daughters, what are you afraid of? Oh don't you hear God saying to Abraham and to you: "Do not fear; I am your protector" [Gn 15:1]. What do you seek on earth, O daughters, if not God? You already possess him. Therefore be firm in your resolutions; stay in the ship in which he has placed you, and let the storm and hurricane come. Long live Jesus!; you will not perish. He may sleep, but in the right place and at the right time he will awaken to restore the calm. Therefore, my daughters, do not fear, you are walking on the sea amidst the wind and waves, but with Jesus.

What is there to fear then? But, if fear takes you by surprise, exclaim strongly with St. Peter, "Oh Lord, save me!" He will stretch out his hand to you; hold it tightly and walk joyfully. Let the world turn upside down; let everything be in darkness, smoke, and noise, God is with us.

"My Crucifixion"

On September 20, 1918, Europe groaned in the last throes of war. At the same time the entire world reeled under a great flu epidemic that would kill millions, including Pio's four-year-old nephew and, three days later, the boy's mother, Pio's favorite sister, Felicita. No one was sick in the remote friary of Our Lady of Grace. There the morning was even quieter than usual since Fra Nicola was out begging and the Superior had gone to another friary on business. Just two years since Pio had arrived at Our Lady of Grace, he was the only adult there that morning. The students were occupied, and Padre Pio was engaged in the occupation that for years now had taken up most of his time: he was praying.

He had said mass and was kneeling alone in the choir loft, as he made his thanksgiving for this inestimable priestly privilege. Before him, just a few feet away, was a big crucifix with Jesus' face wracked with pain and blood streaming from the wounds on his head, hands, feet, and side. A month later, having received a letter from Padre Benedetto ordering him to describe "in detail exactly what happened," Pio would write a letter trying to explain:

What can I tell you in answer to your questions...? My God! What embarrassment and humiliation I suffer in being obliged to explain what you have done to this wretched creature! On the morning of the 20th of last month, in the choir, after I had celebrated Mass, I yielded to a sweet sleep [in fact, this was an ecstasy]. *All the internal and external senses and even the very faculties of my soul were immersed in indescribable stillness. Absolute silence surrounded and invaded me. I was suddenly filled with great peace and abandonment which effaced everything else and caused a lull in the* [spiritual] *turmoil* [of the dark night in which he lived spiritually]. *All this happened in a flash.*

While this was taking place I saw before me a mysterious person similar to the one I had seen on the evening of 5 August. The only difference was that his hands and feet and side were dripping blood. The sight terrified me and what I felt at that moment is indescribable. I thought I should die and really should have died if the Lord had not intervened and strengthened my heart which was about to burst out of my chest.

The vision disappeared and I became aware that my hands, feet and side were dripping blood. Imagine the agony I experienced and continue to experience almost every day. The heart wound bleeds continually, especially from Thursday evening until Saturday. Dear father, I am dying of pain because of the wounds and the resulting embarrassment I feel deep in my soul. I'm afraid I shall bleed to death if the Lord does not hear my heartfelt supplication to relieve me of this condition. Will Jesus, who is so good, grant me this grace? Will He at least free me from the embarrassment caused by these outward signs? I will raise my voice and will not stop imploring Him until in His mercy He takes away, not the wound or the pain, which is impossible since I wish to be inebriated with pain, but these outward signs which cause me such embarrassment and unbearable humiliation.

This time, there was no way Padre Pio could keep the matter quiet. When he regained consciousness from his ecstasy and dragged himself from the choir to his cell, he left a trail of blood. Padre Paolino, the friary guardian, a man who truly loved Padre Pio, had to tell the Provincial.[7] At this time the Provincial was Padre Pio's beloved spiritual director Padre Benedetto. After Pio told him what had happened in the above letter, Benedetto came himself and wrote Pio's second director Padre Agostino the following: "The signs on him are neither stains nor marks, but real wounds which perforate his hands and feet. I have [also] observed the wound in his side, a veritable gash which exudes blood or a bloody humor. On Fridays it's blood. When I saw him for the first time he was barely able to stand on his feet, but when I took my leave of him he was able to celebrate Mass.... When he celebrates Mass, the 'gifts' are exposed to the public as he has to raise his bare hands."

Faced with what he had seen, Benedetto had to tell the father guardian of all the provinces, who is elected to guide the Order and represent it to the church and the world. Down the chain of command came the sensible order to have Pio examined by medical men to make sure that this was not a con, a sign of mental imbalance, or caused by some medical condition. A second command followed: Pio's condition was to be kept strictly quiet, lest Pio become a magnet for both those looking for true signs of the reality of God and those drawn from vulgar curiosity to any kind of bizarre happening or freak show. Both groups could make Padre Pio and the quiet friary's life intolerable.

Medical Analyses

Padre Benedetto, as Provincial, called in a doctor he esteemed as a fine medical man and a person of sense. Luigi Romanelli was head physician at the city of Barletta's hospital. He saw Padre Pio's five wounds in May 1919. Rome was sent the results but objected that Padre Benedetto had a personal relationship with Dr. Romanelli, insulting to the integrity of both men.

In order to obtain a second opinion, Cardinal Merry del Val sent a doctor who, by his own admission, had "no belief in supernatural phenomena," Professor Amico Bignami, a professor of medical pathology at the University of Rome. He studied Pio in June 1919. In October of the same year,

Professor Giorgio Festa, a surgeon in private practice in Rome, made his first examination of the stigmata. Dr. Festa made three examinations of the wounds, the last in 1925. Other doctors who saw Pio's stigmata were Pope Benedict XV's physician, Professor Giuseppe Bastianelli, and Dr. Angelo Maria Merla, a physician who was also mayor of San Giovanni Rotondo. The latter made the very first examination and confirmed that the wounds had nothing to do, as some would claim, with tuberculosis.

Wounds that are deep and not superficial—and these wounds were very deep—either heal up or they become infected with gangrene which, untreated, leads to death. Padre Pio had wounds in the palms of his hands, in each of his feet, and in his side for fifty years. They did not heal until his death and when they did, after half a century, not even one left a scar. Nor did any wound ever become infected.

Padre Pio lost as much as a cup of blood a day. And yet when medicine during Pio's lifetime began doing blood tests, physicians found his blood work "perfect" with "no signs of anemia." This although Padre Pio, who even as a seminarian skipped dinner to pray, ate less and less as he aged, ultimately living on almost nothing while sleeping two to four hours, if that, out of each twenty-four. Much of the rest of his time he worked at a task—hearing confessions—that demanded total concentration.

Doctors Merla, Romanelli, and Festa ruled out that the

wounds were self-inflicted, that they were the result of disease, or that they were physiological evidence of neurosis. Festa and Romanelli concluded, as Romanelli put it, that the wounds constituted "an inexplicable phenomenon for human science alone" and counseled one must be "without fear of moving to the supernatural for their explanation."

Merla, who believed Padre Pio a saint, was a politician. The mayor said simply he didn't know what the wounds were. Bignami had a major problem. His belief system did not accept supernatural phenomenon, so he had to find another explanation for the wounds. Examining Padre Pio, he had been struck by the Padre's simplicity, goodness, and evident integrity. For this reason, he had to rule out that Pio was a con man who wounded himself to become famous. Bignami concluded that the wounds had come about through a limited neurosis and that Padre Pio unconsciously kept them going by disinfecting them with iodine. Bignami was sure that if the wounds were left alone, they would heal.

Bignami ordered that Pio's wounds be bandaged for eight days, with the dressings changed by a group of people, so each could watch the others to verify no one let Padre Pio put iodine on his wounds.

Since Bignami had been sent to Our Lady of Grace by the head of the Holy Office, the local Provincial ordered that the bandaging be done. Here is the report from those who participated:

We, the undersigned, testify under oath, having received from The Very Rev. Father Pietro of Ischitella, the order to bind the wounds of Padre Pio of Pietrelcina, Capuchin priest, and we verify the following: 1) the condition of the wounds during the eight days always remained the same, except on the last day when they acquired a vivid red color; 2) every day, as can be seen from the bandages which we preserve, all the wounds bled, and more abundantly on the last day, so that we were obliged to send him a handkerchief to dry the blood which trickled down the backs of his hands whilst he celebrated Mass. It is to be noted that when we bandaged the wounds, we did not use any medication and, even though we trusted Padre Pio completely, in order to avoid the slightest suspicion, we also took away the phial of iodine that he kept in his room. In faith, etc.

The report is signed Padre Paolino of Casacalenda, Father Basilo of Mirabello Sannitico, and Father Ludovico of San Marco in Lamis.

Dr. Bignami's theory had been blown out of the water. After eight days under wraps, the wounds were bleeding more than ever! Dr. Festa, up in arms at Bignami's imputation that Padre Pio was neurotic and, worse, his statement that Padre Pio was maintaining the wounds unconsciously with iodine, which implies a moral blindness on Pio's part, wrote an entire book on the wounds. He looks at them as a medical man and takes science as far as it can go, that is to a point where, in his view, only the supernatural can offer an explanation.

Dr. Festa insisted that the wounds were neither the result of external trauma nor of the application of powerful, irritating chemicals [the iodine]. He reasoned that the wounds did not show signs of trauma, while the use of chemicals would have been observed in other parts of the body. Moreover, once the wounds were bandaged, the effects of chemicals or trauma would have ceased as the body began to repair itself.

At Festa's last examination, the wounds had been open, bleeding, unhealed, uninfected, and untreated by iodine or anything else for seven years. Before they closed, at the moment Pio's Way of the Cross ended with his death, this time period would stretch to fifty years.

Keeping It Quiet

In his humility, Padre Pio suffered at being singled out this way. He did his best to hide his hands and feet from the spiritual daughters who came to his daily Mass and to his bi-weekly conferences on the spiritual life.

However, it was impossible to hide his hands all the time. After observing him at Mass, the young seminarians at the friary—too new in the spiritual life to appreciate Padre Pio's embarrass-ment—confronted him directly as to what was going on. Their questions ceased when they saw how much they upset him. He begged them not to talk about him but it was too easy to just tell their mothers or sisters. Soon the whole village knew, and word was fast spreading to the nearest city, Foggia, and on to the region's metropolis, Naples.

In Naples, the owner of the secular newspaper heard about Pio's stigmata and commissioned an outstanding writer, a "modern" intellectual—neither a churchgoer nor believer—to travel to Our Lady of Grace and investigate. What was going on in this friary? Chicanery? Dark Age superstition with no foundation in reality? Or something genuine?

Padre Paolino had strict orders to keep quiet. But the naïve Franciscan did not believe this meant he must lie if asked direct questions or refuse Franciscan hospitality to anyone. At that time there were no inns or hotels in San Giovanni. A crowd simply camped out among the goats and sheep as they waited to attend Padre Pio's Mass, have him hear their con-fessions, and pray over their sick. When the noted journalist arrived among them, he asked Paolino to introduce him to Pio. Paolino did so, and Pio, who had no idea who this per-son was, chatted with the journalist about Naples, for which Pio expressed fond memories from his army days. The jour-nalist observed Pio's simplicity, his down-to-earth warmth, and his loving-kindness to all who came to him. The writer was impressed that before him was not a charlatan but a man truly trying to live up to the ideals of St. Francis.

Then a miracle happened in front of the journalist's world-weary eyes. A young man on crutches was told by Padre Pio to drop them and walk.

The man had no faith and protested, "I'll fall." At last, urged on by Pio, he dropped the crutches, but clutched fearfully at the wall to support himself.

"Come on, walk." Pio laughed. Something in that confident laugh caught the crippled man's soul. He let go of the wall. He walked. His foot, mangled in an accident, had been healed.

The journalist interviewed the young man, a cultured fellow whose doctors had agreed the foot required surgery if he were ever to hope to walk again. The young man had come not for himself but for his polio-crippled child. Earlier, when Pio had told the parents to take off her braces, they had fearfully refused. The child was not healed.

"Because of your lack of faith," Pio chided.

After the father's healing, he went back on behalf of his child and was told to keep praying for the child's cure, too.

The article about all this was a sensation, especially because it appeared in a secular newspaper written by a well-known intellectual who had no axe to grind on behalf of Christianity or the Catholic Church.

The resulting publicity which spread all over Italy brought

Pio a great sorrow. The Father General of the Order, punishing Padre Benedetto, ordered him not to let himself be reelected Provincial. Benedetto obeyed, although he had been a fine Superior sure to be reelected. Worse, the Father General ordered Benedetto give up being Padre Pio's spiritual director. This was a terrible blow to Pio, who had found in Benedetto a true spiritual father.

What was so unfair about both rulings is that Benedetto had ordered strict secrecy concerning Padre Pio. After the Naples article, it was he who chided Padre Paolino: "You dare to take the secret of a soul in the fullness of its delicacy and offer it to the newspapers as a news item?" And he ordered again, in the gravest understanding of that word, that Paolino and every friar refrain from all acts that were "harmful to the dignity of the habit."

If Rome blamed the Capuchins for allowing Pio's stigmata to become public knowledge, the Capuchins, in turn, sacrificed Padre Benedetto as the scapegoat. The truth is there was simply no way for Pio's stigmata to remain a secret. The seminarians lodged at the friary alone would have carried the tale. Time would reveal it was God's will for Padre Pio to become a public figure, through whom God would touch and totally change innumerable souls. In that sense, the break between Pio and Benedetto was also used by God to withdraw human support from Pio, throwing the saint more totally on the Lord alone.

Cardinal Merry del Val of the Holy Office, who orches-
trated Bignami's examination of Pio and many other events
that caused Pio suffering over the next years, put it well: "The
Church," he said, "can persecute a saint. That will, after all,
only increase his holiness. But woe to the Church if she
appears to credit a charlatan or does not persecute the false
saint, since these failures would lead many people astray who
are searching for truth and looking to the Church for guidance as to where it is found."

A saintly man himself, Merry del Val did not act out of any
animosity for Padre Pio or for the Capuchins. He knew that
if Pio were a saint, God would look out for him. Merry del
Val's job was to look out for all the people Pio could hurt if
he were a false saint.

The Public Figure

No more than his predecessor could Padre Pietro of Ischitella, Padre Benedetto's replacement as Provincial, stem the human tide engulfing Our Lady of Grace Friary and the young, stigmatized Capuchin. Padre Pietro could try to hold back the crowds by keeping the news out of the Catholic press, but he had no power to keep it out of secular publications.

In his heart of hearts, he did not see this as a disaster. "Perhaps such [nonreligious] newspaper reports," he said, "have made a bigger impression on the public: some graces attributed to the prayers of the good friar feed the faith of believers."

Padre Pietro, who would die five years after his appointment (probably from the stress of his position between Pio, whom he loved, and the dictates of Rome), reported to his Superiors:

Requests for [Pio's] prayers arrive from all over the world, and ... often [later] thanks for graces received. From the furthest regions come visitors who are not guided by unhealthy curiosity, but by a true spirit of devotion. Padre Pio sometimes hears confessions for 16 hours a day. In the warm season there were thousands of communicants daily.... Many people returned to the practice of their religion. There were also conversions to the faith. All this, in my opinion, constitutes the true prodigy, and bears witness to the fact that the Lord desired to reveal, this, His chosen one for the good of souls and the glory of His name.

Pio and Two Popes

Even as the Holy Office kept pressure on the Capuchins to stifle this Padre Pio business, Pope Benedict XV, well informed by clergy and his personal physician who had visited Pio, judged the stigmatic one of those "truly extraordinary men whom God sends on earth every now and then to convert sinners." When a monsignor openly criticized Pio, Benedict wrote him, "You are certainly badly informed, for which I order you to go to Padre Pio in order to convince yourself of the lack of charity and of your error." When Benedict died January 22, 1922, things got much worse for Padre Pio.

The new Pope, Pius XI, a very learned man, had a much different opinion of Padre Pio because he was told many lies about the young Capuchin, who had some true enemies. Who were these enemies? Sad to say, among them were the priests of San Giovanni Rotondo who did not like seeing their church practically deserted while the villagers rushed up the hill to attend Mass at the friary. They had already resented Pio's "stealing" the young women, to whom he was giving spiritual direction and conferences even before his stigmata drew the world to his door.

These worldly priests could have pulled their parishioners home by becoming holy themselves. Instead they turned to the local bishop, a man whose life and motives regarding Pio, like theirs, would not have borne scrutiny. This bishop sent a formal petition to Rome against Pio. It was full of untruths, including that the friars were using Pio to collect money from the ignorant and credulous. That June, the Holy Office ordered Pio be moved from Our Lady of Grace to some remote friary where the crowds could not find him.

Pio held obedience in such high esteem that he could say, "*For me the voice of my Superiors is the voice of God*" [which had never kept him from arguing with Benedetto like any son with his father over the latter's directives]. Informed now, he replied he was ready to leave at once.

But the removal, ordered and tried repeatedly over the next few years, proved not so simple. Cynics could claim it was because Pio had put San Giovanni Rotondo on the map and had already begun providing livelihoods for the locals who were renting out their beds and serving meals to the visitors. The more pious, like Pio's spiritual daughters, insisted it was because they weren't about to lose the blessing of having a saint in their midst to shrive their sins, marry, christen, bury, and otherwise lead them to God.

In either case—and probably both were involved—whenever someone arrived who the people of San Giovanni Rotondo thought might have come to transfer Pio, local menfolk took up arms and surrounded the friary. One wild young man actually pointed a gun at Pio and said, "Try to take him and he's a dead man."

For Pio to leave Our Lady of Grace simply proved impossible.

Pio's Feelings

Padre Pio loved the simple people of San Giovanni Rotondo and promised them that, if he had to leave and it was left up to him, he would have his body sent back for burial among them. It was his nature to want to upset no one, to give everyone who wanted him as much of himself as he could. But he did not, in another sense, think much about himself at all. He was too busy with the long confessional lines, full of people waiting for him. He professed to be *"weary ... and immersed in extreme grief, in the most hopeless desolation, in the most ago-nizing affliction, not because I fail to find my God but because I am not winning over* [to God] *all my brothers."*

Yet as early as June, 1919, nine months after receiving the stigmata, Pio wrote to Padre Benedetto, *"I haven't a free moment.... Innumerable people of all classes and of both sexes come here for the sole purpose of making their confession.... There are some wonderful conversions."* In his own soul, Pio experienced both *"great spiritual joy and great spiritual desolation"* at once.

As for the stigmata, he had asked repeatedly to suffer so that he might be associated with Jesus' work of redemption of souls. But he had hoped to suffer unseen, unknown. As Padre Paolino wrote in his memoirs, Pio never talked about the wounds, unless ordered to do so. "On the contrary," noted Paolino, "he did all in his power to conceal God's gift, by trying to cover his hands with his habit before he took to wearing gloves."

New Restrictions

In June 1923, under new orders from Rome, Padre Pio began saying his daily Mass in an interior chapel privately, that is with no one present. The thirty-five-year-old Capuchin also had a new order: to no longer reply, either himself or through another person, to any of the many letters seeking graces, advice, or anything else.

Since his arrival at Our Lady of Grace in 1916, Pio had written hundreds of letters, giving spiritual direction to many souls serious about spiritual advancement. This would now cease. That same afternoon, about three thousand inflamed locals swarmed into Our Lady of Grace to protest losing the padre's Mass. Through their mayor, they had also sent a protesting telegram to the ecclesiastical authorities. In the face of this angry mob, the friary Superior had no choice but to promise that Padre Pio would once more be celebrating Mass the following morning in public.

Not too much later, Rome pushed again for transfer. A police official arrived to see how the police might help carry it out. He met Pio, who professed himself willing to go but begged the official *"to act with insight, not for me, but I would not want those poor people who are trying to make me stay in San Giovanni Rotondo to be hurt."*

When word got out of the police official's presence, a mob once again descended on the friary. With the help of the mayor, the police official convinced the crowd he was not there to take Padre Pio away, so he escaped. But his subsequent report warned that there would be no transfer of Padre Pio without bloodshed.

Caught between a rock and a hard place, Rome insisting Pio be transferred and the locals insisting they would keep him, dead or alive, the poor Provincial died of a heart attack. His assistant became the new scapegoat. As if the Provincial and his assistant had been preventing the transfer of Pio, the assistant would not succeed the Provincial. Instead, a Capuchin from another province would be brought in to "solve things."

The Odor of Sanctity

Among the accusations during the first decade after Padre Pio received the visible stigmata was that he—most unsuitably for a friar—used perfume. In time it became understood that what people sometimes—not always—smelled around Pio was not something from a bottle: it was instead often an odor emanating from his blood. Dr. Giorgio Festa, who wrote extensively from firsthand study on the stigmata of Padre Pio, once took cloths saturated with blood from Pio's stigmata wounds with him when he drove back to Rome. Blood rapidly becomes putrid with a foul odor but for a long time these cloths gave off a wonderful perfume that filled not only the car Festa drove but also the office in Rome where they were stored.

Naturally-inexplicable perfumes also seemed to indicate the unseen presence of Padre Pio among his many spiritual children by the phenomena of bilocation. One of Pio's converts, for instance, after meeting the stigmatic, adopted the habit of beginning work at his typewriter with the sign of the cross. One day when he forgot, he immediately smelled an odor for which he could find no natural cause. He recognized it as a smell connected to Pio and told his family, most of whom smelled it too, that the Padre had "come" to give him a friendly reminder not to forget to pray when he started to work.

This phenomenon, known as the odor of sanctity, was not, in Pio's case, always the same. Some people, even at the same moment, smelled a flowery perfume, others smelled incense, others "fine tobacco," and still others nothing. Whatever the odor, it always heralded some grace given through the prayer intercession of Padre Pio. A nun, for instance, who had written the overwhelmed stigmatic priest twice about some concerns without receiving an answer, woke one night to this odor. She immediately sensed that Pio was there in some way, assuring her that he had taken her prayer requests to heart. From that moment, she felt herself borne along on a great current of peace—a grace much more important than the perfume that had signaled it.

Years later, after his death, testimonies of favors and graces received by people who asked Padre Pio's prayer intercession would sometimes mention wonderful perfumes that had no possible human source.

Pio's Undying Love for His Family

When Padre Pio began life at Our Lady of Grace Friary, he never again returned to live in his beloved hometown of Pietrelcina but he did not lose touch with his family. On his returns to Our Lady of Grace from military service, he liked to travel via Pietrelcina and, in 1918, with permission, he returned home to escort his youngest sister Graziella to Rome when she entered the Briggitine Order. (Of course, this was before the stigmata made him a prisoner of the people of San Giovanni Rotondo.)

Pio's letters to his parents are filled with gratitude and profound love for them. Here is a sample:

My dearest parents,

Easter is coming up and I seem to hear a voice in my heart that reminds me of all the gratitude I owe you, who have been and always will be the persons most dear to me. And now I want to wish you a long and prosperous life, blessed with every heavenly and earthly gift. This and no other is my prayer which in these days I petition to the risen Jesus and hope He accepts and approves with his blessing.

So, I sincerely hope that you will not be like those Christians who make the whole of Easter consist only in sensual pleasures, because this is entirely contrary to the spirit and law of Jesus Christ. I urge you instead to never cease to advance along the ways of God, remembering that sooner or later we will have to present ourselves before the tribunal of God.

With this end in view, then, I urge you not to forget the Easter precept, the sole means that restores our health. For this, I ask you to please let me know who at home fulfills their Easter duty.[8]

The whole religious community send their greetings. Please embrace for me grandmother, the professor, my uncles and aunts ... and their families. And lovingly embrace for me all my sisters, my brother, and sister-in-law. Lots of love from your son, Fra Pio.

"Take Good Care of My Son"

Having heard wild tales of Pio's "wounds," in April 1919, Pio's parents, along with their son's wife (the one who had hired a brass band for his ordination), came to the friary to see for themselves how "Franci" was doing. Delighted to find him looking healthy and jovial as ever, they returned home reassured.

Since Pio could no longer go to visit them, from then on "Zia [Aunt] Peppa," as Pio's mother was called, would come from time to time on visits to San Giovanni Rotondo. Once she stayed forty-four days so that her granddaughter,

Giuseppina, who was with her, could benefit from the mountain air. On December 5, 1928, Padre Pio's spiritual daughter, the American Presbyterian-born Mary Pyle, who had built a home very close to the friary, visited Pietrelcina and returned bringing Zia Peppa, who wanted to spend Christmas near her priest son.

That Christmas there was a biting wind and bitter cold as, unusually, snow fell, but the saint's mother refused the warm wool dress she was given because she was afraid to look as if she were pretending to be "a lady." Her own clothing was entirely too light for the fierce winter; after attending Padre Pio's Christmas Mass, his mother returned to Mary Pyle's house and went to bed with double pneumonia.

Padre Pio visited her repeatedly, accompanied by his Superior, who gave Padre Pio's mother Communion. It was the Superior, Padre Paolino, to whom she had said on her last visit to the friary, "Father guardian, take good care of my son, Padre Pio." Pio gave his mother the last sacraments on January 3, 1929. Then he kissed her, gave a deep sigh, and fainted.

They laid the saint on a bed next to his mother's, and when he came to, he wept copiously as his mother quietly died. Pitifully Pio lamented as he wept, *"Oh my little mother, my beautiful mother."*

Finally someone uncomfortable with all this emotion said, "But dear father, you yourself teach that suffering must not be anything other than an expression of love which we must offer to God, so why are you crying?"

"But these are precisely tears of love and nothing other than love," Pio answered.

Rome Tries Again

In March 1931, Rome decided that "the Padre Pio problem" needed correcting at the lowest level: The Superior of Our Lady of Grace Friary should be changed, and a Capuchin from northern Italy, that is another province, be brought in to replace him. This was to be done secretly but at once the whole village was talking about it. Those southern Italians agreed they were not about to have their friary taken over by a "foreigner," that is, an Italian from some other place.

When a friar minor arrived at the friary to spend the night on his way back from preaching a Lenten sermon, the town rose as one. About a hundred men, boys, and those crazies [these were not Padre Pio's spiritual daughters] the friary derisively termed "the holy women" pounded in the friary door—using a lamppost as a battering ram—and demanded "the stranger" whom they were determined to run out of town, at least as far as the city of Foggia.

Facing the mob alone, the Superior courageously refused to turn over the friary's guest. But he let Padre Pio come to the window with the poor "stranger," who was, according to the friary annals, more dead than alive with fright. This gesture was intended to demonstrate that Pio was not in any danger. Afraid Pio was speaking only under obedience, the group posted a guard around the friary while the rest went home to bed. "I don't know how we can carry on like this," the beleaguered friary Superior ended his report to the Provincial.

In the end a compromise was reached: The intruders would not be prosecuted, the local Capuchins would try to ensure that their Order sent no "foreigners" to rule the friary, and the poor visiting Franciscan got out alive!

A Long Retreat

In June 1931—eight years after the first order of this kind had been thwarted by a mob descending on the friary—Rome ordered Padre Pio to stop saying Mass in public. At a time when he was making great headway in bringing souls to his beloved Jesus through hearing confessions and giving spiritual direction, Pio was also ordered to cease both ministries. He was not even to hear the confessions of his fellow friars.

The Superior had the miserable job of telling this to Pio who, the Superior knew, would obey but suffer. Pio's only reaction was to look toward heaven and say, "*May God's will be done.*" But he had to cover his eyes to hide his tears. The Superior tried to comfort him, but if Pio found comfort, he found it in no human words or gestures but only in prayer. He retired immediately to the choir before the large crucifix, and remained there until well after midnight.

This "imprisonment" lasted two years. As far as Pio knew at the time, it might last his entire life. Yet, he remained docile, never saying a word of complaint. When others brought up the restrictions and tried to console him, not once did he offer the slightest criticism of those who had taken away the exercise of his priestly vocation despite three apostolic visitations by Holy Office investigators, each one carrying only praise for Pio and the friary Capuchins back to Rome.

His public ministry might have come to a standstill but no one could prevent Pio from continuing to work for souls: he simply shifted to offering up these sufferings and to intercessory prayer. Under obedience, he had learned to keep his public Mass to perhaps thirty-five minutes. Now, saying Mass privately, he could commune with Jesus as long as he wanted and his Mass usually went three hours; on Christmas Day, it lasted five. Daily, an hour of thanksgiving followed. Later each day, another hour passed in mental prayer in the choir. Then, having spent much of the day talking with God, he went to the library to read and study about him. Afternoons, after joining the community in prayer at vespers and an hour of adoration, he returned to devout reading until evening, then back to the choir for another two hours of prayer and finally, at a very late hour, to bed. It is no exaggeration to say he was now a living example of St. Paul's exhortation "to pray always," for in between the many other hours of prayer, no matter what else he was doing, his lips were always moving and the rosary beads slipping between his fingers.

As always, prayer drove out other appetites. He skipped breakfast and supper and barely ate at midday. A seminarian of those days, Carmelo Durante recalls, "I would see everyday the Padre seated in the refectory who, instead of eating, would gaze up in ecstasy at the painting of Saint Francis that then hung above the entrance to the pantry. The pressing and energetically repeated entreaties of our director of college, Padre Girolamo da Rotondi, were necessary to make him return to himself and convince him to take a mouthful."

His continued copious bleeding from the stigmata was evidenced in the stained gloves, socks, and heart-wound wrappings which he turned in to the Superior under obedience. The suffering from the wounds was visible by the way he moved on his wounded feet, stepping with great difficulty. About these sufferings—as about every suffering—he remained silent.

Changes

Encouraged by his new secretary of state Eugenio Cardinal Pacelli [later Pius XII], in March 1942, Pius XI sent a fourth pair of investigators to report on Padre Pio. That June the archbishop who had conspired against and lied about Pio was removed from his office for that and other serious offences and a new archbishop appointed.

In July, Padre Pio was informed he could once again say public Mass. He cut the Mass down to forty-five minutes and added a half hour to his hour of thanksgiving. He was still unable to hear confessions until the following year but the people flocked just to attend his Mass. A priest from Bavaria spoke for many when he said, "On attending Padre Pio's Mass, I saw Jesus Christ on earth come to life again after twenty centuries."

The following year, 1943, at age forty-seven, Padre Pio was finally back in full apostolic harness.

An Evildoer?

Even at this time, when he had papal approval, some were still accusing Padre Pio of wickedness. Anonymous letters claimed he was violating his vow of poverty and taking money from visitors. Other letters claimed Pio let women into the friary late at night for nefarious purposes.

The answers to the charges against poverty are found in the diary of Padre Pio's spiritual director, Padre Agostino. The diary explains that Pio told his confessor of having on occasion received money from someone seeking to make restitution [probably for stealing]. "Sometimes he had to pass a sum of money from one person to another, as the person who was giving the money could not find anybody else trustworthy. On other occasions, he had recommended needy people and offerings [for them] were given to him by many because they wanted to remain anonymous." Agostino ends his diary entry by saying, "I am convinced, as I was at the outset for that matter, of the Padre's uprightness as regards poverty." Indeed anyone who knew Padre Pio knew that the riches he coveted were not human ones, while any money given him went right on to someone in need.

As for the anonymous letters about the handsome Pio and women, these accusations were also proven false by his friary Superior. That good man, trusting Pio completely, still exerted himself to get up at night and check on the doors. He even applied paper "seals" to them, so if they were opened during the night, the paper would tear.

It always remained intact.

On Fridays, especially during Lent, Padre Pio often went down into the empty, locked church at night to make the Way of the Cross. When an anonymous letter again accused Pio of letting women into the church at night, the Superior, ignoring intense cold to do his duty, crept noiselessly into the church on freezing bare feet and hid behind the door to spy on Padre Pio.

The Superior writes: "To my surprise and great humiliation, I heard the poor Padre who was calumniated so much by souls who had sold themselves to the devil, beating himself and saying the 'Misere'[9] in a clear voice. It was a great consolation for me to personally ascertain the Padre beating his poor, innocent flesh to the shame of those who hurled the vilest calumnies against him." The next day when another anonymous letter arrived, the father guardian threw it in the trash.

A Teaching Tool

In spite of his true love for his fellowmen, Padre Pio could raise his voice or strongly rebuke certain people who came to him, according to many witnesses. When Pio did such things, explains Brooklyn-born Padre Joseph Pius Martin, who lived with Padre Pio the last years of the saint's life, "It was a teaching tool."

The saint, his fellow friar points out, often had only a minute or two, sometimes less, with a person. By his charism of the word of knowledge, he knew with whom to be tender and with whom a rebuke would have a better effect. The goal, Padre Joseph Pius insists, was always to work on a soul toward its salvation, not any ego needs or pique of Padre Pio's. Pio, the same witness points out, never refused to take on anyone as his spiritual child except for those cases where he knew a refusal would goad the individual into needed remorse, change a sinful state of life, or bring about other improvement.

Padre Pio was aware of those who wanted to become his spiritual children without investing any personal effort, who planned on having the saint "do it all" for them. But he would accept even some who were questionable characters or of weak motivation, only remarking, "Now don't make me lose face!"

Others insist that Padre Pio's brusqueness was a personality trait that persisted in spite of his efforts to tame it. Most likely there is truth in both views.

His Brusqueness Puts Her Faith to the Test

Angela Morano Rispoli of Calabria writes:

I met Padre Pio in 1939. I was very young, had lost my father, had many family problems and had to choose the companion of my life. Having heard of the friar with the stigmata who lived at San Giovanni Rotondo and of his prodigies, I decided to consult him ... in this difficult choice. Together with my brother and his wife ... [I arrived at San Giovanni where] there was only one board-inghouse.... The owner received us affectionately, encouraging us to trust in Padre Pio who was enlightened.

...We went to the friary to the Mass that the Padre said at 5 A.M. The little church was packed, mostly with men.

Padre Pio's Mass! It is not possible to describe the concentration, his suffering face, his tears that made one think he was in touch with the supernatural. On the faces of those present one could see wonder, amazement and emotion!

After Mass, Padre Pio heard confessions. My turn came. Trembling, I went down on my knees and after having accused myself of some sins, the Padre interrupted me and continued to make a list of the sins I had committed.

He gave me absolution and I said: "Padre, I would like your advice. Several young men have asked for my hand in marriage, but I am afraid to choose. Please help me!" He replied, "Do you think that I am a fortune-teller? Pray to the Holy Spirit for enlightenment," and he closed the little door.

His reply upset me. I burst into tears and ran to the boardinghouse to tell the landlady who had so encouraged me to confide in the Padre. She comforted me affectionately saying that Padre Pio was often brusque but if I insisted I would be helped. The next day I was again in front of the confessional, waiting my turn, but this time too, it didn't go well. As soon as the Padre saw me he shouted: "You here again!" and he sent me away.

Disappointed but trusting in our Lord, who probably wanted to put me to the test, I said to myself "Tomorrow is my last day at San Giovanni. I will try again and hope not to be disappointed."

In fact I went again and when my turn came, great was my surprise. The Padre had changed completely. He was smiling and said: "What do you want, my daughter?" Encouraged by these words I took the sheet of paper where I had written the names of my suitors, hoping to be able to read them, but the Padre didn't give me the chance to open my mouth. He simply said: "Go for Rispoli, but you must let me meet him."

Having established her faith in God, Pio had given her advice. Here is how it turned out. Rispoli she had never met. He was a lawyer working in Asmara, Ethiopia [today Eritrea], whose mother had approached Angela about marrying her son. Although Angela's own mother had no faith in going by advice from some friar, Angela waited months until Rispoli returned home. They met, and he seconded his mother's proposal. When she said he must meet Padre Pio before she could decide, he was astounded but agreed. In his testimony, he explains that he had received a good Christian education but the death of his father while the son was in Africa, unable to help, had "shaken me considerably and cooled my faith."

Arriving at Our Lady of Grace, after Mass, Giovanni Rispoli was one of a troupe of men who followed Padre Pio into the sacristy, lining up to kiss his hand. As Rispoli approached, Padre Pio—who had no way to know who this stranger was—looked him in the eye and said, using the affectionate diminutive form of the stranger's name, "You, too, Giovannino, have landed here?"

The young religious doubter was so shaken he fell to his knees and asked to go to confession. He confided to Pio that he could not resign himself to losing his father.

"Continue on the straight road," encouraged Pio, "and you will find him again."

Rispoli testifies: "His words sank into my soul and gave me relief." After his confession he told Padre Pio that his mother had introduced him to a girl and wanted him to marry her.

"Can't you see," Pio responded, smiling, "that you were made for each other?"

The young man had other concerns. World War II was about to break out. As a draft officer, he could be called up. He had no job unless he went back to Africa. Padre Pio dealt with all these questions saying that a job would come, that war wouldn't touch him, etc. These predictions proved precisely true: Giovanni was called up but was away; another officer was sent in his place. He never went to war; he got a job in Italy.

Married in 1940, Angela and Giovanni were happy, but doctors told them they could have no children. They returned to Padre Pio yearly, and when they told him they could have no children he replied, "They will come. Prepare the bonnets. Prepare the swaddling bands. The first will be boys, the rest girls."

In 1943 doctors told Angela, who was in severe pain, that she needed surgery. They went to Pio. "Surgery? Who must tell you that you are pregnant?" Pio growled.

A delighted Giovanni asked Padre Pio if they should name the baby after him. "The first ones you can call what you like. You will give my name to the last one," Pio replied.

After three boys, when she was forty and the youngest six, Angela again seemed ill. She wrote to a friend in San Giovanni, asking her to talk to Padre Pio on Angela's behalf. He told this woman, "I am seeing to the Signora Rispoli's illness." Again it proved to be a pregnancy, and a girl was born in October, 1956. Six years later, at forty-seven, Angela gave birth to another girl, which they named Pia.

Angela emphasizes that throughout the thirty years Pio guided their lives through his God-given gifts, Pio's prophecies to her and her husband—whether given brusquely or with fatherly tenderness—always proved correct.

A Man Who Laughed

All his life Padre Pio was known among his friends as a man with a good sense of humor. Playing pranks on his sisters and fellow novices, and later making his Capuchin brothers laugh by telling innocent little jokes and stories during recreation, Padre Pio fulfilled the paradox that a follower of Christ must both "pick up [his] cross and follow me" and be filled with "the joy of the Lord."

Here is a story someone took down during the friars' recreation period, in which Pio speaks of himself in the third person, then switches to the first, as he tells a tale from his brief military career:

> *It was his turn to go somewhere.... Our soldier courageously armed himself with an umbrella and, well protected, he went on his way along Piazza Plebiscito* [in Naples].
>
> *"Hey, soldier," but the soldier went straight on as if he hadn't heard anything.*
>
> *"Hey, I'm talking to you, soldier." It was a Colonel who, justifiably, was becoming impatient. He had to turn back.*
>
> *"What kind of thing is this?" roared the Colonel under the rain that was drenching him. "A soldier with an umbrella! Have you gone crazy?"*
>
> *I offered him my umbrella* [saying] *"If the Colonel wants to protect himself, I will accompany him...."*

> *The Colonel realized he was dealing with a dull recruit and with a gesture of annoyance, turned away from me and left me there with my umbrella in my hand.*

Another war story Pio liked to tell was the one of the guileless recruit and the WWI sergeant who was preparing the troops for a visit by the king of Italy. The sergeant knew that the conversation between the king and any given recruit usually followed a formula.

First question: "How old are you?" He practices this with the recruit, who answers, "Twenty-two."

Second question: "How many years have you been in the army?" Again he practices with the recruit to reply, "Two."

Third question: "Whom do you serve more willingly, your king or your country?" To this the recruit is to reply, "Both."

After much practicing with the three questions and their proper answers, the day arrived at last. The king came and inspected the regiment. He began with the questions—but changed the order in which they were asked.

"How many years have you been in the army?" he says. "Twenty-two," replies the guileless recruit, following the learned response.

"And how old are you?"

"Two."

At this point the sergeant breaks out in a cold sweat as the king frowns and exclaims impatiently, "Either you're stupid or I'm stupid." And the recruit, rejoicing at knowing the right answer replies promptly, "Both, Your Majesty."

Pio's jokes could be made about things like drunkenness too. He would stand up to imitate a drunk trying to hang on to a wall and walk when he told the following: "The drunk saw a millipede walking along a wall and said to God, 'Why, Lord, have you given a thousand feet to this little animal and I can't even hold myself up on two?'"

World War II

Padre Pio saw wars as God's call to humanity to repent and think of their souls, but he still suffered with those suffering in both the First and Second World Wars. Italy was dragged into the Second World War through Mussolini's relationship with Hitler. But after Mussolini was hanged and the Fascists overcome, Italy changed sides. German soldiers became not allies but invaders, and American forces landed to drive them from the country.

During this period American pilots stationed at Bari were bombing parts of Italy held by Germany. Foggia, the closest city to San Giovanni Rotondo, was 90 percent destroyed by American bombing. Padre Pio assured the people of the little city of San Giovanni Rotondo—through his presence there it was no longer just a village—that they would not be bombed.

But in August 1944, it is said that the Americans heard a rumor that there was an ammunition dump in San Giovanni Rotondo and sent out a fleet of planes from Bari to bomb the town.

Before the planes arrived in San Giovanni, they faced a friar in the sky who signaled them, "Go back!" Faced with this extraordinary intervention, the squadron leader led his planes to drop their bombs over the Adriatic before returning to base. Some of the squad, it is said, visited Padre Pio and affirmed it was he they saw in the sky.

Padre Joseph Pius Martin, who relates this story, says that so many people attested to this incident that years later the Capuchins tried to get the report filed by the returning airmen as to why they failed to make their assigned drop in San Giovanni Rotondo. (When bombs were not jettisoned over target, a report had to be filed.) But the friars did not succeed.

A Far-Traveling Man

For roughly fifty years Padre Pio was unable to leave the friary, lest the local people take arms to keep him there. Yet, he continued to appear at various places around the world, including the battlefront. The testimony of Maria Pompilio of San Giovanni Rotondo:

I was near the door ... to the right of the main altar. By my side was a man who looked fixedly at Padre Pio as he removed his vestments, and he said breathlessly: "Oh God, yes it is him, truly him; I am not mistaken!" And when the other men began to disperse, this man threw himself at Padre Pio, fell on his knees crying and with his hands joined, said: "Padre Pio, thank you for saving me from death; thank you...." And the Padre, putting his hands on the man's head said: "You must not thank me, my son, but Our Lord and the Virgin of Graces." Padre Pio then went to the choir to pray.

The man went into the corridor, where he was stopped by three or four other men, who asked him why Padre Pio had said what he had said to him. I was also present in the corridor and the man told the following story: "I was a captain in the infantry, and one day on the battlefield, during a terrible hour of fighting, a little distance away from me a delicate, pale friar with beautiful, expressive eyes, who was not dressed as a chaplain but as a simple friar, hurriedly and gently called me saying: 'Captain, move away from that place; come to me quickly.' I ran toward him and had not even reached him when, in the place where I had previously stood, a grenade exploded, opening up a pit. If I had been there, my body would have been blown into the air in shreds. I wanted to thank the little friar who had called me, but he was no longer there;

he had disappeared without my realizing it and even though I looked around for him, I never saw him again.

"On the same day, another colleague of mine told me a beautiful monk had saved him from danger of death, and other soldiers in the Italian base said they had seen a friar among them who looked toward heaven and prayed. One of these soldiers said it was Padre Pio who had been on the battlefield.... More out of curiosity than faith, I wanted to come here to see.... Now I know that it was precisely him whom I saw on the battlefield.... I am happy to have been able to thank him personally and to kiss his holy hand."

There were other similar stories. One was told by a lawyer from Rome. The only son of a lawyer and a schoolteacher, he was fighting in Libya as a lieutenant during the terrible Battle of Tobruk. Seriously wounded but conscious, he became aware that a line of English tanks were moving toward where he lay, unable to move. When one of the armored vehicles was only a few meters away from flattening him, a chaplain dragged the lieutenant to safety.

The young man survived and eventually returned to Italy. He never forgot the chaplain, however, and always longed to be able to thank him. One day he found his devout mother reading a book and there was a photo of the priest who had saved him. It was Padre Pio.

Obtaining leave, he traveled to Our Lady of Grace, but when he saw Padre Pio surrounded by so many people, he became shy. He said to himself he would come back another time when he had a longer leave and speak to Padre Pio then. But as he prepared to leave, Pio called across the sacristy, "Mario, ... now that you have found me you are leaving without saying 'hello'?"

The crowd parted to let the dazed young man through. With a few words encouraging him to practice his religion, Padre Pio hugged the young man whose life he had saved. That was the start of a long relationship, with many trips by the lawyer to San Giovanni Rotondo.

Through his prayers and the sufferings he offered up, Padre Pio obtained the safety of the whole Gargano Mountains area and many soldiers. Father Damaso of S. Elia a Pianisi, father guardian at that time, recalled once when Pio went twenty days living on the Eucharist alone, without food or *water*. Medically speaking, going so long without water is impossible—dehydration and death would normally ensue. This, and other sufferings the guardian describes, Pio specifically offered God, begging him, says the Superior, "to save the Gargano from the disaster of the war."

While Pio was certainly not omniscient, he often seemed to know the condition of people who were far off. Thus, many came to ask him about missing loved ones during the war. To one person he said, "Perhaps you will have a letter soon." Returning home, a letter arrived saying the missing combatant had been captured and was in England safe and sound. A mother was told, "Oh, how he suffered but he is all right now." News soon came her son was dead. To a third person Pio remarked that he hadn't seen the person "on the other side" [of life], and the person turned out to be alive.

Among the war dead was Padre Pio's "black sheep" sister Pellegrina. Injured in the January 1944 bombing of Chieti, a town where she was working, Pellegrina died a month later in the hospital, but not before she had called for a priest and received the sacraments. Padre Pio's prayers and sacrifices for Pellegrina had seemed a failure for thirty years but prevailed in the end.

Pio Predicts Future Events
by Divine Inspiration

Padre Carmelo Durante witnessed various examples of Padre Pio's gift of prophecy. Carmelo testifies:

During the last world war, I would spend the summer holidays from the Gregorian Pontifical University of Rome—where I was studying—at San Giovanni Rotondo close to my spiritual director Padre Pio.

It was the summer of 1942. Naturally we spoke about

the war every day and particularly of the resounding military victories of Germany on all the battlefronts.

I remember that one morning I read in the friary parlor in the newspaper the news that the German advance troops were already approaching Moscow.

I was amazed and saw in the news flash, the end of the war with Germany's final victory. Going out into the hallway, I met the Padre and, delighted, said to him: "Padre, the war is over! Germany has won!"

"Who said so?" Padre Pio asked.

"Padre, the newspaper!" I answered.

And Padre Pio: "Germany won the war! You listen to me, Germany this time will lose the war and worse than last time! Just remember that!"

"But, Padre," I responded. "The Germans are already approaching Moscow!"

"Just remember what I told you!" he repeated.

I insisted, "But if Germany loses the war, it means that Italy will lose, too!"

And he answered me with decision, "Well, we will have to see if we finish the war together."

These words of his were totally obscure to me at the time, given that Italy and Germany were allies; but the following year they became clear ... [when Italy made peace with England and America and then declared war on her former ally, Germany].

Another day in the friary hallway Padre Pio said to me, "Italy will lose the war out of the mercy of God, not because of his justice."

And I appealed ... "But Padre, how can one lose a war out of mercy and not out of justice?"

He responded ... "Yes, it is as I say, Italy will lose the war out of the mercy of God, because if she won the war with Germany, the war over, Germany would crush Italy under its feet." And he stamped his food on the ground with force to bring across what that meant.

Later it became clear to me how losing the war for Italy was really a victory and not a disgrace at all, but a grace.

Not Only the Future of Countries

As far back as 1922-23, when Mussolini was dismissing railway and other workers, Padre Pio's first spiritual children in San Giovanni were talking about a certain father of a family who, having lost his job, was forced to beg.

Padre Pio commented, "You'll see, Mussolini won't die in his bed." Twenty years later, Mussolini would be hanged by his own people.

Roughly forty years later Pope John XXIII died, and the conclave was assembling to elect a new pope. The friar aiding the then-aged Padre Pio badgered the saint so much to know who would be elected that Pio finally snapped, "Montini, now leave it alone." Cardinal Montini, of course, became Paul VI in that papal election.

Prayer, Always Prayer

Capuchin Eusebio Notte witnesses:

> One evening when we were in his cell ... the discussion turned to the Rosary. To provoke Padre Pio into telling me how many rosaries he had said that day [I told him I had said three rosaries of five decades and said, "How about you? Forty?" To which Pio replied,] "I have said sixty of fifteen decades but keep it to yourself!"
>
> On that day alone he had said 60 complete rosaries, which means 180 of those we usually say.... [Then] you think that he carried out that activity which we all know, ... hours of meditation, three or four hours of confessions, many hours for Mass, with preparation and thanksgiving, people who continually besieged him ... and so on—then we are astounded and wonder how this man managed to say so many prayers. This is a question for which I have never found an answer!

The Prayer Groups

In 1943, as the war was at its deadliest, Pius XII sent out a heartfelt appeal for people to gather in groups and pray. Padre Pio took the pope's call to heart and thus were born the Padre Pio prayer groups—simple get-togethers for the sole purpose of prayer under the direction of a priest. This undertaking spread all over the world. At the time of Pio's death, there were 726 prayer groups in 20 countries, with a total membership of just under 70,000 members.

True prayer always leads to deeds of charity. Members of these prayer groups became particularly involved in the charitable works promoted by Padre Pio. In the early years after Pio received the visible stigmata, these charities were fairly informal—help with food, medicines, clothes, and rent money for the poor, ill, and needy of San Giovanni; the placement of poor, abandoned girls from the surrounding villages with groups of nuns; placement of war orphans; help for unmarried mothers; jobs and skills training for adolescents; and restoration of harmony in troubled families.

The Home for the Relief of Suffering

Padre Pio truly longed to come to the relief of anyone who suffered. In 1925, with the help of charitable donors, he was able to open a small hospital in San Giovanni named for St. Francis. There were two wards, each with seven beds—one ward for men and one for women—and two private rooms. But in 1938 an earthquake damaged the building so badly that the hospital closed its doors.

Two years later, in January 1940, Pio formed a committee to build a bigger hospital across from the friary, which he called "The Home for the Relief of Suffering." Three doctors took part in that meeting, as did a laywoman. As the meeting concluded, Pio reached in his pocket and took out a coin someone had given him. "I want to make the first offering for the home," he said and handed it over.

From that moment, offerings began to pour in from all over the world. Particularly the prayer group members and other spiritual children of Padre Pio gave generously toward making the padre's dream of help for the sick a reality. But it would still take years to bring the work to completion. The cornerstone would not be laid until 1947, two years after WWII ended. When the first patient was finally admitted in May 1956, Padre Pio rejoiced. That year, on the feast of Corpus Domini, he went to the home with a procession of Jesus in the Blessed Sacrament. In the visitor's book, he wrote that day, *Veni, vidi, et exclamavi: benedictus Deus qui facit mirabilia magna solus* ["I came, I saw and I exclaimed: blessed be the Lord who alone does great and marvelous things."]

In addition to the huge hospital, there are also Padre Pio

Centers for handicapped children—twenty-two of them by 1968—and a Padre Pio Center for the Blind. Twenty years after Padre Pio's death, the Handicapped Children's Center in San Giovanni Rotondo, located just behind the friary, was home to 1,830 handicapped children cared for by the Capuchins.

Pio's final charitable undertaking was the Home for Old and Infirm Priests. Sometime between 1953 and 1959 the saint got the idea for this when he considered that, unlike the Capuchins, who had each other's help in old age, diocesan priests often had no one to assist them in serious illness or the infirmities of age. This project was not finished until after Pio's death.

That Medicine Be "Truly Human"

Many years later, at Pio's beatification, Pope John Paul II commented on The House for the Relief of Suffering:

> He [Pio] wanted it to be a first-class hospital but above all he was concerned that the *medicine* practiced there would be *truly "human,"* treating patients with warm concern and sincere attention. He was quite aware that people who are ill and suffering need not only competent therapeutic care but also, and more importantly, a human and spiritual climate to help them discover

themselves in an encounter with the love of God and with the kindness of their brothers and sisters. With the House for the Relief of Suffering, he wished to show that God's "ordinary miracles" *take place in and through our charity.*

Directing Lives

Many lives were given a special focus through the counsel of Padre Pio. Besides Angela Rispoli, who needed help to choose a husband, another typical example is the testimony of Nicola Vecere. Nicola felt he had a vocation to become a Salesian priest in the well-known order given to youth work. But he got sidetracked for a while, studying for another religious order until overwork made him drop out for a rest. Before he could return to take religious vows, he was summoned by the Fascists to military service. After thirty-nine months in the army, he was released in August 1945, from a prisoner-of-war camp in France.

Once again Nicola felt the call to the Salesians but he decided to seek the guidance of that well-known director of souls, Padre Pio. He traveled from his hometown of S. Elia a Pianisi to Our Lady of Grace and went to confession to Pio. Padre Pio assured him that Our Lady was guiding him to the Salesians. He also assured him that he would succeed in becoming a member of this order.

With the promise of Pio's prayers, the ex-soldier entered

the Salesian novitiate. Things did not go well for him. It appeared he would not be allowed to stay, but in the end, another fellow who had gotten him in trouble was dismissed, and he was retained. After four years of studies, Nicola returned to see Padre Pio, who again encouraged him that he would make perpetual vows one day.

However, after the six-year trial period, Nicola was *not* permitted to make final vows. His faith was shaken. Had Padre Pio been mistaken? Suddenly everything turned around: The Provincial of the Salesians, who had rejected Nicola, suddenly died. The new Provincial who replaced him told the rejected Salesian not to go away and not to lose hope. Shortly after, he accepted Nicola Vecere permanently into the Salesian order.

Padre Pio and a Young Pole

When World War II ended, in 1945, a young Pole, who had done his priestly studies in secret right under the eyes of Poland's Nazi occupiers, came to Rome for post-ordination studies. Father Karol Wojtyla made a pilgrimage to San Giovanni Rotondo and went to confession to Padre Pio.

According to Padre Joseph Pius Martin of Our Lady of Grace Friary, Wojtyla has countered the claim that Padre Pio told him at that time that he would be pope one day. But whatever their exchange, Wojtyla left San Giovanni Rotondo confirmed in devotion to Padre Pio as a great man of God.

Fifteen years later, the Polish priest was a bishop spending a lot of time in Rome for the Second Vatican Council. True to his vow of total poverty, at this time Padre Pio had given The Home for the Relief of Suffering to the Vatican. Weekly, a layman employed by the Vatican came to San Giovanni to meet with Padre Pio regarding the hospital. In Rome, Bishop Wojytla asked this layman, Angelo Battisti, if he would take a note to Padre Pio. The note the Polish prelate handed Battisti asked Padre Pio's prayers for a friend of the Bishop's—a laywoman. The mother of four girls and a concentration-camp survivor, she was dying of terminal cancer.

When Battisti gave Padre Pio the card, the Capuchin read it and remarked, "We cannot refuse him."

A few days later, Bishop Wojytla sent a second note with Angelo Battisti to Padre Pio. Written by hand on a little white card, the note thanks Padre Pio on behalf of himself, the cancer patient, her husband, and her daughters for her complete cure.

Padre Pio told someone, "File away those cards." So, surmised Padre Joseph Pius, Padre Pio must have known what lay in the future for Poland's brilliant young bishop.

As Pope John Paul II, Wojytla remains devoted to Padre Pio. He visited San Giovanni Rotondo again as a cardinal and, later, as pope. And it was he who beatified Pio, with thanks to God for that privilege.

As for the two little white cards that mark a miracle, they are housed today in the archives at San Giovanni Rotondo.

Papa Forgione

Padre Pio's beloved American spiritual daughter, Mary Pyle, built a house very close to the friary. It was there that Padre Pio's mother had died. After Mama Forgione's death, Padre Pio's father came to live permanently with Mary. In his last days "Zi Grazio" ["Uncle Grazio"], as most people called the affable, devout old man, became bedridden. As October 1946 opened, the nearly eighty-six-year-old's condition deteriorated.

On October 4, Pio was hastily summoned from the friary. He spent the night at Orazio's bedside and was a constant visitor the next few days as the thread of his father's life frayed irreparably. A photo of the time shows Padre Pio tenderly spooning soup into his nearly-comatose parent. As with his mother, when the moment of death came, the saint sobbed copiously. Better than anyone, he knew that he owed his vocation to this humble farmer and workman who had traveled across the seas repeatedly to an alien land—where Italians and Catholics were often despised and sometimes seriously mistreated—to earn, by backbreaking menial labor, the money that permitted Francesco to study and become Padre Pio.

His father was buried October 8, and Padre Pio's grief was such that he took to his bed, getting up only to celebrate Mass daily, until October 14. His spirit, as always, was resigned to God's will, but in the flesh he was sad and depressed. On October 15, he was finally able to return to the confessional.

The Gift of Reading Minds

Among Padre Pio's many gifts, testifies Capuchin Eusebio Notte, "One which stood out was his capacity for reading other people's minds—naturally, when the Lord permitted him to do so!" Notte continues:

One evening after Benediction, Padre Pio had withdrawn into his cell ... and I was waiting for him in the corridor. At that moment one of our brethren came along and showed me a cardboard box containing some undershirts, which he then went to give to Padre Pio. Shortly afterwards another person entered the cell and I saw him come out immediately with that same box.... Inside myself I felt a surge of rebellion and thought: "He scarcely has time to receive something and he has already given it away! And yet this time it was something that he himself needed!" I had hardly finished thinking ... when Padre Pio called me to accompany him to cell number one where he slept.

I entered the room and he said, *"In that box was a large image of the Infant Jesus which I have sent to one of the patients; the undershirts ... that you wanted are there on the bed!"* and he pointed to ... where the linen I had wanted for him was still lying!

I leave you to picture how I felt!

A Miracle for the Miracle Worker

In 1959, exhausted from forty years of bearing the stigmata while laboring incessantly to bring souls to God, Padre Pio was hospitalized in The Home for the Relief of Suffering. Serious pleurisy necessitated extracting pleural liquid a number of times. Padre Pio begged Padre Agostino to get Rome's permission for his leaving the hospital so he could die in the friary. This was granted and Pio returned to the friary July 3. On August 5th, while he was still ill, the statue of Our Lady of Fatima, which was on pilgrimage in the area, was brought to San Giovanni Rotondo.

When the statue of Christ's mother arrived at Our Lady of Grace, Pio was in bed praying. But the next day shortly before the statue took its leave, Pio had himself carried down on a chair to the old sacristy during the "farewell" Mass. After Mass the statue was carried into the old sacristy and Padre Pio bowed his head, with his ever-ready tears of devotion. He kissed the statue of Mary—she who had appeared to him so many times—and put a rosary he had blessed in the statue's hands. Carried back to his cell, he was so exhausted it was feared he would collapse.

While Pio returned to bed, the statue made the rounds of the wards of The Home for the Relief of Suffering before a helicopter arrived to take it on to its next stop. Testimony of what next took place is from the account of eyewitness Father Raffaele of S. Elia a Pianisi:

Padre Pio expressed the desire to salute the Madonna once again ... and so he was brought into the choir of the new church on a chair once again and he looked out of the last window to the right.... Amidst the shouts of the masses, "Viva! Viva!" the helicopter rose ... but before taking its course, it circled the friary and church three times in order to say good-bye to Padre Pio.

And he, on seeing the helicopter take its leave with the Madonna on board said: "Madonna, my mother, you came to Italy and found me ailing; and now you depart leaving me ill." Having said this he bowed his head, while he shuddered from head to foot. Padre Pio obtained the grace he asked for and he now feels well. He wanted to celebrate Mass in the church the following day but everyone dissuaded him.

In the meantime, however, Professor Gasbarrini [M.D.] arrived providentially; he meticulously examined Padre Pio and found him clinically cured. Thus he told all those priests present, and I am among them: "Padre Pio is well and he can celebrate Mass in the church tomorrow." What a joy this was for us and for everyone!

In short, the news spread that Our Lady of Fatima had given life to Pade Pio once again, and from that day he took up his apostolic activities once again; Mass and confession as in the past. There were some jarring voices that wanted to deny the miracle but Padre Pio would say: "I know whether or not I am cured and whether it was a miracle by the Madonna or not." ... And from that day on, every time he told of this prodigy he could never finish the story without starting to cry.

A Heart of Gold

Padre Pellegrino of S. Elia a Pianisi, who had the joy of living at Padre Pio's side, speaks of Pio's "heart of gold."

Padre Pio's heart!... I am unable to describe the gentle harmony that God's Spirit breathed within him. To me, he was an eternal child, rejoicing in the surprises that were brought to him, from the taking of tobacco to being offered a chocolate. He enjoyed the delicate pleasures of friendship, purified and assured by poverty. He was most sensitive to the slightest courtesy, which he repaid with prayers and graces for eternal life. He was most acute of mind and with the sensitivity of a mimosa. He perceived from a distance the desires of men, and replied to those who loved him, with immediacy. Even the Friary dog was aware of this: if he found the door ... open, he would take a walk as far as Padre Pio's room, scratch a moment near the door and would only go away when Padre Pio said: "Beh, that's enough now, you can go."

Padre Pio had a heart of gold, even for those (and perhaps even more) who received a roar [from him]. His sense of goodness and humanity which shone in his eyes is difficult to explain with words.

A True Son of St. Francis

Like the earlier stigmatic who founded the Franciscans, St. Francis of Assisi himself, Padre Pio loved nature. There are many stories of the way nature returned Pio's regard. One first-person testimony comes from radiologist Dr. Nicola Centra, who one day in 1956 was in the friary garden while Padre Pio was visiting there with some of his many friends.

According to Centra, birds of every kind began to land in the garden and sing, whistle, chirp, or trill as suited their kind. Centra noted blackbirds, sparrows, goldfinches, and other types. Finally, when the noise made human conversation completely impossible, Padre Pio turned his gaze upward toward the creatures perched all over the garden trees, put his finger to his lips and murmured, "That's enough."

Centra says, "The effect was like pouring water on a fire...; a silence like that of a cathedral descended."

Padre Bill

William "Bill" Martin was born to Catholic parents in the undertaking business in Brooklyn, New York—people with close connections to a religious order, the Carmelites, whom they had assisted to settle in the area.

By 1959, when he was a young man, Bill Martin had heard about Padre Pio, "the priest with the stigmata" from a seminarian friend. Planning a visit to Europe, Bill knew whom his Catholic travel agent meant, then, when the agent said, "And don't you want to visit the priest with the stigmata?"

"Sure." Bill shrugged. He was, he says, at that time a "Sunday Mass" kind of Catholic. ("And usually late for that," Bill adds.) To him, a priest with the stigmata, he explains, was like the Eiffel Tower—just another one of Europe's "attractions."

Arriving in San Giovanni Rotondo, however, the young New Yorker experienced such a powerful attraction to the mountain village—which had absolutely nothing to offer the visitor except the physical presence of Padre Pio—that when he left at the end of his short visit, he reshuffled his itinerary to fit in another two-week stay.

Five years later, around 1963 or 1964, when Bill was twenty-five, he returned to San Giovanni, this time wrestling with the possibility that he had a vocation to the religious life. Padre Pio was now elderly, and Bill knew that when he left

Our Lady of Grace Friary this time, he probably would not see the saint again. Perhaps for this reason, the young American began to feel he should stay on at the friary for an extended time. In his indecision, someone counseled Bill to ask Padre Pio if this was the will of God.

Padre Pio's reply was short and to the point: "You *must* stay here."

So Bill stayed about a year and a half in San Giovanni Rotondo, living on an inheritance. At the end of that period, he asked Padre Pio if he thought it OK for Bill to go to the Holy Land.

"Yes," Padre Pio answered, "but remember that's where Our Lord suffered."

Traveling in the Holy Land and then on to Ephesus, Athens, and Cairo, Bill was troubled by a restless lack of peace until he returned to San Giovanni Rotondo. At that time, 1965, he told Padre Pio he thought he had a religious vocation.

"If you have a religious vocation," Padre replied, "follow it as soon as possible."

Bill realized that Padre Pio's tactful reply left him free to decide for himself if he did have a vocation or not. In order not to pressure him, no one told him that Padre Pio said to Padre Eusebio about Bill, "He *must* stay here." After his own discerning, Bill joined the friary community as a Third Order Franciscan on September 15, 1965. Thus he shared the saint's life during Padre Pio's last three years, part of that time assisting him with his physical needs as Pio became more and more feeble.

Bill had consecrated himself as a young man to Our Lady, and all the great graces of his life had always come to him through the Mother of God. Ruminating on those facts, one day he asked Padre Pio to whom did he owe the great grace of a vocation to religious life—to Padre Pio's prayers or to Our Lady?

"Our Lady," Pio replied.

This humility, says Padre Joseph Pius—the former Bill Martin—was typical of Padre Pio. Of living side by side with Padre Pio, Padre Joseph Pius says, "After the timidity wore off, you lived a very simple daily life with this great saint because, in his profound humility, he had no airs or assumption of graces. He never made you feel inferior to him nor ever asked for anything special. He was a lovely person to live with."

All About Love

Yet, in regard to Padre Pio's "wonderful ease and charity with his brothers," Padre Joseph Pius wants something appreciated. "Padre Pio was not acting out of an overflow of joy." As the vice postulator for the beatification, Father Gerard di Flumeri and others have affirmed from formal study of Pio, the saint's entire adult life was lived in the dark night of the soul.

Mysteriously blind to his own virtues and giftedness, Pio never knew if he were doing the will of God. As much as he did to bring souls to God, Pio worried that he might not be doing enough. This although he slept only two hours, Bill points out, retiring at midnight and up for another day of service and prayer at 2 A.M. with only a brief afternoon's rest.

Padre Eusebio, who was about twenty-seven, had been sent to Ireland to study English so he could assist Padre Pio with his correspondence in this language. Upon his return, Padre Eusebio was helping Pio in the latter's cell when Padre Pio suddenly said he wanted to go to confession. Feeling his youthful lack of experience, Padre Eusebio wanted to beg off, worrying, "What if he asks me something about mystical theology?" But Padre Pio launched into the penitent's opening prayer: "Bless me, Father, for I have sinned...," and the young friar was stuck. To Padre Eusebio's surprise, Padre Pio, as he confessed, burst out weeping.

Immediately, Padre Eusebio wanted to console Pio that he had not done anything so bad but Padre Pio countered, *"Listen, my son, you think, like many others, that sin is the breaking of the law, but it's not that but infidelity to love."*

To Be Faithful to Love

Trying to be faithful to love, Padre Pio arose by 2:00 A.M. or earlier to begin praying. He said Mass at 5:00 A.M., followed by at least ninety minutes of prayer in thanksgiving for Mass and Communion. As long as his health permitted, he spent up to nineteen hours a day in the confessional.

In the 1950s the sacristan of that era recalled that penitents had to take a number and wait, often days, for a turn. That same sacristan remembers a day when Padre Pio had heard confessions all day when, just as his workday ended, a busload of pilgrims arrived, seeking the sacrament from Padre Pio.

"Bring them in," was Pio's heroic response. He heard the entire busload of people, one by one.

In his lifetime of eighty-one years it is estimated Padre Pio heard around a million confessions.

At the end of his life, recalls Padre Joseph Pius, even the couple hours of sleep he usually allowed himself often eluded Pio, who became an insomniac.

His health, so bad when he was young that he was expected to die many times, stabilized for a time after he received the visible stigmata. Then it declined again, until in his last years he suffered from asthma that eventually affected his heart. Many nights pain forced him to sit up in a chair, waiting for dawn. He used the time to pray and prepare for Mass and Communion.

He also became increasingly anemic, although his blood count had held up for many years in spite of the daily blood loss. Padre Joseph Pius cites, as evidence of the anemia, the stigmata scabs, which were dark red in Pio's prime years but which in his final days were a pale pink, indicating, says Padre Joseph Pius, Padre Pio had almost no blood left.

Pinned to the Cross

In spring 1957 when Pio's ministry was flourinshing and he appeared to enjoy the esteem of the whole world, from peasants to the reigning Pius XII, the Brother assigned to assist Pio with various daily tasks had "a strange and terrible" dream. "He saw Padre Pio, advanced in years, really old, motionless, ill, withdrawn and senseless; while at the same time he saw higher up another Padre Pio, like a being floating on air without a body, smiling and surrounded with light really glorious and in sharp contrast to the first Padre Pio ... weighed down with years and illness." This dream so distressed the Brother—who believed it a prophetic look at the weight of many crosses to come to Pio in his last days—that he burst into tears, rose from his bed, rean into the chapel and pleaded for an hour with God to let these future sufferings fall on him instead of Pio. Then he went back to bed. He said nothing to anyone but when he went to assist Padre Pio the next morning, the saint took him tenderly in his arms, kissed him, and said "Thank you, my son, for what you did for me last night."

But God did not choose to transfer Pio's crosses to the heroically-charitable Brother. After the flourishing decade of the 1950s, in Pio's last decade, the 1960s, many suffereings, as the dream had foretold, pinned Pio to the Cross. Following years of freedom under Pius XII, there was a new investigation of Pio and his ministry ordered by newly-elected John XXIII who was reacting to real abuses by some of those around Pio[10] as well as to mis-truths he was fed. This inquiry which lasted from July-September 1960 culminated in new restrictions which were only lifted by John's death and the election of Paul VI in 1963. Besides this humiliation, one after another of Pio's closest friends died, including Padres Agostino and Benedetto, as well as Pio's spiritual daughter Mary Pyle and his only, older brother Michele.

The only Forgione sibling left alive was Graziella who had been in far-away Rome as Sister Pia since 1918 and so hadn't really spent time with her brother for nearly forty years. When Sister Pia's Order was led into many excesses after Vatican II, Pia and another Briggitine sister moved out. To Pio, who believed in "obedience, no matter what!" this was anathema. The siblings met to hash it out. They ended exhausted but neither had changed position. They did not meet again in this life and Pio suffered true agonies over what to him was Pia's "desertion" of her order.

Physically, he was failing, too, due to dreadfull asthma

attacks that took their toll on his heart. A tiny elevator had to be installed so the friars could get him up to his room using a wheelchair. In the midst of all these final trials, the devils harassed him with new fervor, sometimes throwing the frail, old saint bodily to the floor.

Brotherly Love

All his life Pio —who suffered so much himself—had great compassion for the suffering. The great visible work of his life would be the model hospital he insisted be called The Home for Relief of Suffering. With his Capuchin brothers, too, he was often moved to intercede. On April 14, 2000, this writer, visiting Our Lady of Grace Friary and enjoying a cup of tea with Padre Joseph Pius, was introduced to a still-living example of Pio's fraternal charity.

About 1950, Brother John Sammarone was so ill with tuberculosis that his doctors told him he must prepare to die. Brother John told Padre Pio, who dismissed the terminal verdict with a lighthearted, "Oh well, they're doctors!" Then Padre Pio asked Brother John whether another fifty years of life would do him. Brother John says he thought another fifty years was a fine idea. He did not died, and fifty years or so later, in the year 2000, was looking quite robust.

Come, Sister Death!

Even before his ordination, Pio often longed for death in order that, in the words of his favorite saint, the apostle Paul, he "might be dissolved and be with Christ." Yet death eluded him until he entered his eighties. Like many a saint before him, near the end at least—and perhaps much earlier, if his prophetic remarks to a fellow seminarian are considered—Pio had precise foreknowledge of his death date. He told a blind disciple named Petruccio that he would die in his eighty-first year.

To his niece, Pio remarked in 1966, when he was seventy-nine, that he "wouldn't be here in a couple years"; but she naively thought he meant he'd be transferred at long last from Our Lady of Grace Friary. To others he remarked casually that he'd die when the crypt of the new (that is the second) church was blessed.

Due to the huge crowds, the tiny friary church had eventually been replaced with a larger one. At that time the crypt was left unfinished. Then, when the Superiors were about to build elaborate outdoor Stations of the Cross for the meditations of the many pilgrims, someone complained, "We really should finish the church first." So work resumed on the crypt in 1968. When it was complete, a visiting Franciscan Superior from Rome blessed it on Sunday morning, September 23, 1968.

That night, Padre Pelegrino was on duty with the very frail Padre Pio, who was now eighty-one. After 1:00 A.M. Padre Pio wanted Pelegrino to hear his confession. He told Pelegrino, "You will say Mass for me today." Even at that hour there were pilgrims outside. Padre Pio walked to the veranda and blessed them. Then his strength failed and he had to get in his wheelchair. Doctors Gusso and Sala were hastily summoned, one of whom later commented, to attend "the sweetest death I ever saw" as Padre Pio simply stopped breathing at 2:30 A.M.

The Resurrection Life Begins

Shortly before Padre Pio died—his time of suffering over and his time of glory approaching—the stigmata he had borne for fifty years showed their first change. The father guardian at that time notes in the friary chronicles that "they gradually began to close, and the bleeding diminished, until they appeared at his death completely healed and without any scars. Proof of this lies in the fact that, precisely at the last minute [of his life], the last scab or pillicle on the left hand detached itself."

In what was another miracle, Dr. Giuseppe Sala writes:

Ten minutes after his death, Padre Pio's hands, thorax, and feet were held up by me ... and were photographed by a friar in the presence of four other confreres. The hands, feet, [and] thorax ... showed no signs of wounds; nor were scars present on [any] ... areas where during his life, he had well-defined and visible wounds. The skin on the above-mentioned areas was the same as that on the rest of his body: soft, elastic, and mobile.... These wounds which Padre Pio had had during his life, and which disappeared on his death, must be considered to be a fact beyond all clinical behavior and of a supernatural nature.

"What Will We Do Without You?"

Toward the end of his life, people used to ask Padre Pio, "What will we do without you when you die?"

"Go before the tabernacle," was Pio's reply. *"In Jesus you will find me also."* A fitting reply for a man of God whose whole life had been with Jesus, in Jesus, and for Jesus.

Aftereffects

There were many who said that as soon as Padre Pio died, San Giovanni Rotondo would become a ghost town. And yet, more than thirty years after the saint's death, his tomb attracts people with the same magnetism that once drew them to the living Capuchin. On a typical weekday, a long, never-ending line of humanity oozes slowly under its own mass through the public parts of the friary past Padre Pio's room [today looked into through a glass wall], bunches up as it traverses the narrow choir loft where he received the stigmata, and falls to its knees in the crypt before Pio's tomb.

In one year, 1997, 6.5 million people visited that tomb. The next year, 1998, on the twentieth anniversary of his death, 70,000 people crammed together to celebrate the occasion. A third, much larger church, is under construction to accommodate the crowds that only increase each year.

When Pio's heroic virtue was recognized through his formal beatification by Pope John Paul II on May 2, 1999, St. Peter's Square was prepared with 150,000 seats and standing room for another 100,000. Since even this number was insufficient, another 100,000 witnessed the ceremonies and Mass on huge screens set up in St. John Lateran Square, through permission of the mayor of Rome. Pio's was probably the largest crowd ever assembled for a beatification.

Rather than dwindling numbers after Pio's death, more letters than ever are received at the friary. Coming from all over the world, they request Padre Pio's prayer intercession for graces of every kind. And God seems to honor many of the requests. Other letters, often from people who previously wrote to request prayers, gratefully report receiving favors that range from relatively small things—such as finding a job or settlement of a lawsuit—to "impossible" cures from last-stage terminal illness or dramatic rescues from certain death.

The Beatification Miracle

Mrs. Consiglia De Martino was a member of one of the Padre Pio prayer groups founded by the Capuchin saint. Because she was devoted to Padre Pio and lived not too far away from San Giovanni Rotondo, Mrs. De Martino used to go once a month to Our Lady of Grace on pilgrimage to the tomb of Padre Pio. On October 31, 1995, this housewife and mother, having made some strenuous exertions, felt a sort of "tear" in her chest and on the left clavicular region. This was accompanied by a strong sensation of discomfort and pain. When she woke the following morning, her neck had a growth on it the size of an orange.

Frightened, she summoned her brother-in-law, since her husband was away. He took her to the emergency room of the Riuniti Hospital in her hometown of Salerno. As soon as she arrived there, Mrs. De Martino began invoking the prayers of Padre Pio. Dr. Ferdinando Basile immediately ordered a scan, which showed there was "an effusion of non-emetic liquid that came from the upper clavicular to the kidneys." The diagnosis was that there had been a traumatic rupture of the thoracic duct in the neck and that surgery would be needed.

Meanwhile, a daughter of the patient telephoned to ask prayers of Fra Modestino, a Capuchin at San Giovanni Rotondo who had been a confrere of Padre Pio and was a friend of the De Martino family. A little later, from the hospital Mrs. De Martino herself phoned Fra Modestino, who encouraged her that she would be remembered during the evening Mass at Our Lady of Grace.

Fra Modestino went at once to the tomb of Padre Pio and prayed with great faith for Mrs. De Martino's cure. He asked Padre Pio to intercede before God with confidence because his old friend had promised him that, in heaven, Pio would always get favorable answers from God for Modestino's prayer requests.

That was borne out. The Italian mother and housewife woke in the hospital the following morning and found that while not yet treated, the tumefaction of the neck had disappeared and the swelling had almost completely gone. The entire problem was resolved within twenty-four hours. On November 3 an ECO of the abdomen and an X-ray of the thorax showed nothing abnormal whatsoever. Two days later, on November 6, Mrs. De Martino was released from the hospital.

A panel of five physicians summoned by the Congregation of the Causes of Saints reviewed the medical data and the testimonies of the fifteen witnesses—family members, acquaintances, medical personnel, and doctors. The five physicians agreed with complete unanimity that the diagnosis was well-established and the cure very rapid, complete, lasting, and scientifically inexplicable, especially considering that no pharmacological therapy or surgery had been involved.

In fact, it was because she had had no treatment whatsoever that Mrs. Martino's cure was singled out from many more dramatic ones. In her case there would be no need for the Congregation of the Causes of Saints' medical experts to try to untangle the supernatural from the pharmacological or other therapeutic efforts. Today when most people are rushed into treatment or immediately medicated, that is a rare situation.

A Few Samples

The Friary of Our Lady of Grace puts out a monthly magazine which features writings by Padre Pio, reminiscences of him, and testimonies from the letters arriving at the friary relating, the recipients maintain, graces received through the prayer intercession of the dead saint. Here are (some of them condensed) a few samples:

> In May 1986 I suffered a heart attack. The doctors in the hospital had given up hope of me ever recovering. As I lay dying in my bed, a lady ... gave me a novena leaflet with a relic of Padre Pio. When I just finished the prayer ... I suddenly felt warm hands on my chest and the smell of roses. The burning feeling seemed to go out the window.... I knew I was cured. When the doctor examined me, he told me I was cured.

> My wife and I recognized the holiness of this man [Padre Pio] twenty-seven years ago during and after the crisis of my daughter's affliction.... She had been in a coma and paralyzed about thirty days.... After extensive tests it was confirmed she had tetanus.... We were told that the situation was grave and to prepare for the worst. The paralysis was affecting her ability to breathe. She became critical. Her convulsions were so severe that the Sodium Seconal injection was given at the rate of one grain per minute. The doctors and nurses that monitored the medication thought she could not survive. Two other persons, an adult and a child, died from the same condition about the same time. She was confirmed and given the last rites. Someone heard of our plight and wrote Padre Pio.

We received a letter from him, saying, "Have faith, I spoke with the Lord and He will grant you your daughter...." After July 30th our daughter awoke as if from a deep sleep....

I am 56 years of age. During the years 1960-76 I suffered from severe depression, diagnosed as manic. My family was all deeply upset as it was pronounced to be incurable. During my last visit to a hospital in 1976 a patient placed the little leaflet with the third class relic on it in my hand. I said the prayer then and there although I did not know anything about Padre Pio. I have never since suffered from depression.

I have a nephew who had been born blind. The doctors said he would never see. I asked Father Fanning if I might have one of Padre Pio's relics for a short time. He lent it to me and I applied it to the baby's eyes. In about two weeks, we noticed that he was following objects. His parents took him to the eye specialist, who said the child could see but he had no medical explanation for why.

Christmas Eve 1983 my car died. It was really hard for me as a single parent of three not having a car.... I couldn't afford a loan for a car so I prayed to the Lord, along with the prayers for Padre Pio's intercession.... One of my sisters said to be specific in prayer ... so I prayed for a dependable

car. (I liked little red sports cars with black interiors)....
Anyway this past Christmas I ran into a friend ... [who]
felt led to give me her extra car.... She signed the car over
to me in January. And you know what! Praise God, it is a
dependable car, but also a red car with black interior. We
laugh but I know the dear Padre helped me.

Padre Pio! You were a man so filled with compassion, you
promised to wait at the door of Paradise until the last of your
spiritual children was safely inside. Like your favorite saint,
the apostle Paul, you fought valiantly to pull souls from darkness into the light of Christ. And, like Paul, you bore in your
own body "the brand marks of Christ" willingly suffering
pain in order that you, as Paul said of himself, might aid the
redemptive work of the Savior.

Pray for us, great friend of Christ that we, too, may reject all
darkness. May your example of total surrender to God inspire us.
May your prayers obtain for me the grace of _____
and help me please God by _____. And may you
one day, with Jesus and all his saints, joyously open for me the
door to Paradise!

To become a spiritual child of Padre Pio
contact Our Lady of Grace Friary
71013 San Giovanni Rotondo
FG, Italy

Other books by Patricia Treece
with information on Padre Pio:

Nothing Short of a Miracle
(chapters on his healing charism)

The Sanctified Body
(his odor of sanctity, Near-edia, bilocations,
and other bodily mystical phenomena)

Apparitions of Modern Saints
(some of his after-death appearances)

Quiet Moments With Padre Pio
(a selection of the saint's writings)

Notes

1. *Send Me Your Guardian Angel* by Father Alessio Parente O.F.M. Cap. (editions Carlo Tozza, Napoli, December 1984) is over two hundred pages long.
2. There are three major Franciscan orders: the original Friars Minor, the largest, and two "reforms" of which one is the Conventuals (distinguished visually by black habits) and the other the Capuchins (distinguished by their pointed hoods).
3. Until ordained priests, the young Capuchins were called Frater, which means "Brother."
4. Displays like this were common in even American religious houses well into the twentieth century, their purpose being to visually remind onlookers "that thou art dust and unto dust thou shalt return," as a goad to living for eternal joys, not temporal ones.
5. Rather than a vision, a locution is confined to hearing words which may be spoken aloud or heard in the soul.
6. This was not to commit suicide but to psychologically let go of life which, it is said, may cause physiological death. Pio was so obedient that if his spiritual directors had given permission, he might well have died at this time.
7. Capuchin friaries in an area, termed a province, are all under an elected board of directors headed by an elected Provincial.
8. The Catholic Church's rule that every Catholic should go at least once yearly to confession and Communion.

9. A prayer begging God's mercy on a sinner, a sign of Pio's great humility.

10. John was especially upset by hearing of those local women—these were not Pio's spiritual daughters—who rushed into the friary church for his morning mass hollering and physically assaulting others to get the best seats while an aged friar, who was slipping into senility, shouted back at them with the same loss of control and dignity.